childmade

childmade

Awakening Children to Creative Writing

Cynde Gregory

Station Hill Press

Published by Station Hill Press, Inc., Barrytown, New York 12507.

Grateful acknowledgement is due to the National Endowment for the Arts, a federal agency in Washington, D.C., and the New York State Council on the Arts, for partial financial support of this project.

Produced by the Institute for Publishing Arts, Barrytown, New York 12507, a not-for-profit, tax-exempt organization.

Cover design by Susan Quasha.

Distributed by the Talman Company, 150 Fifth Avenue, New York, New York 10011.

Acknowledgements:
"The Heaven of Animals," copyright ©1961 by James Dickey: reprinted from *Drowning With Others* by permission of Wesleyan University Press. This poem originally appeared in *The New Yorker*.
"A Death Song," copyright ©1982 by Claudia Lewis: reprinted from *A Big Bite of the World* by permission of the author.

Library of Congress Cataloging-in-Publication Data

Gregory, Cynde.
    Childmade : awakening children to creative writing / Cynde Gregory
       p.   cm.
    Bibliography: p.
    Includes index.
    ISBN 0-88268-093-5.— ISBN 0-88268-088-9 (pbk.)
    1. Creative writing (Elementary education)   I. Title.
LB1576.G77 1989
372.6'23—dc20   89-11452
                                       CIP

Manufactured in the United States of America.

For
Helen Elam, who taught me to think
Michael Rutherford, who taught me to teach
Gene Garber, who taught me to write
and for the kids

Contents

Preface

The poems and stories contained in this book are the original creations
of children with whom I have worked during the past ten years. All are
first drafts, composed in the classroom during my visit. I have a tendency
to pounce upon a brilliant work only seconds after it first appears on
paper, and beg for a copy to call my own. For this reason, you may notice
an occasional skewed phrase or an inconsistancy in terms of logic.

With some trepidation, I have chosen to correct spelling. It is my
assumption that the writers intended for their words to appear in their
culturally agreed-upon form, i.e., spelled "correctly." I have, however, left
syntax and punctuation alone. An odd twist of language can both reflect
the way the young writer perceives the world and simultaneously contain
the folkways of her voice.

Whenever possible, the entire poem or story is included. The few
instances in which an excerpt is given are marked parenthetically as such.

Some of my students are girls and some are boys. Because I am
unwilling to assume that all third persons are boys, and because referring
to the wonderfully creative people upon whose work I have based my
book as "it" seems rude, I have solved the problem of gender reference
by alternating he with she. I tried to maintain relative balance and favor
neither sex. In an earlier version, I attempted the visually bulky s/he, but
the repeated appearance of the word in the text struck me as not unlike
the experience of walking through a heavily fenced pasture at midnight
without benefit of the moon.

Most of the work contained in this book was a direct outgrowth of residencies under Alternative Literary Programs in the Schools. ALPS is a six-day writer-in-residency program supported in part by the New York State Council on the Arts, the National Endowment for the Arts, the New York Foundation for the Arts, and The New York State Writers' Institute. If you are interested in having an ALPS writer visit your school, contact the director, Michael Rutherford, at RD 1, Indian Ledge Road, Voorheesville, NY 12186.

I wish to express gratitude to everyone who supported me in the writing of this book. Deepest thanks to:

Michael Rutherford, director of Alternative Literary Programs in the Schools (ALPS) who has employed me, defended me, patiently listened to various ideas in late night long-distance phone calls, and been my best professional friend for the past ten years.

Mary Strange for her clear sight and gentle suggestions; Donna Prizgintas for her brilliant ideas; Chuck Ver Straeten for the faith; Nancy DeNicolo for basic upkeep and reality checks; Joel Schuman for gentle reminders that computers have feelings, too.

Mary Ann Ronconi, Len Michon, Jim Powers, Dick Martin, Jerry Griffith, Teri Udell, and Kathe Hartnett.

Teachers Mrs. Bennett, Ms. Browne, Mrs. Briscoe, Mrs. Pavlovic, Ms. Murphy, Mr. DiGorgio, Mr. Hyatt, Mrs. Naughter, Ms. Gardner, Mrs. Beck, Mrs. Kasch, Mrs. Conlee, Mr. Brennan, Mrs. O'Conner, Ms. Rosano, Mr. Meisel, Ms. Pechenik, Ms. Kelly, Mrs. Tuller, Mrs. Wheeling, Ms. Semmler, Ms. Pierson, Ms. Schiesz, Mr. Hart, Mr. Appel, Ms. Daly, Mrs. Laakkonan, Mrs. O'Brien, Mr. O'Dell, Mrs. Reed, and Mr. Huggins, whose students provided the poetry and stories contained in this book; and my sincere apologies to anyone whose name has inadvertently been left out.

Woodstock, Academy of Holy Names, Central Valley, New Berlin, North Rose, Perry, Tesago, and Voorheesville Elementary Schools, as well as the Woodstock Children's Center, the Beacon City Schools, North Babylon Union Free School District, the East Greenbush School District, and the Rensselaerville Institute.

ALPS, The New York State Council on the Arts, the National Endowment for the Arts, the New York Foundation for the Arts, the New York State Writers' Institute, and Poets and Writers, for financial support.

Everyone at Station Hill, especially Cathy Lewis.

And finally, and most especially, to all the kids who continue to teach me those things that are most important.

Introduction

This book contains the reflections of a subculture whose rich literary expression is all but ignored. Too often, a child's writing is cherished solely for the glimpse into an innocent life we adults recall with nostalgic longing. But children's writings, like children's lives, are infinitely more complex, more deeply felt, and more richly embroidered than the simple, sweet surface would lead us to believe. These are writings about rejoicing and grief, solitude and communal ecstasy, rage and peace, self-hate and self-acceptance. They are more than poems about feelings; they are pieces of literary art, conscientious, serious, and exquisitely beautiful.

This book has been created to help adults navigate the inner terrain of children's creative writing process. Children who learn to embrace and cherish their visions through language learn as well to cherish the written word in all its forms. Possessing the written word as something of their own making enables children to proceed with greater courage and passion through the manifold experiences their lives will hold. From their poems and stories, we can come closer to knowing them and to knowing ourselves; for what they write about are not things of childhood, long gone from the lives we now lead, but things of the heart and of the human spirit.

1

Beliefs, Techniques, Tools

Traveling the Inner Terrain

The fact that you have picked up this book and are reading it proves that we believe the same thing: in order to be the best possible teacher you can be, you must always remain a student. Knowledge is a relationship between you and your experiences. You have to constantly make yourself modest, place your little self in perplexing and fascinating situations, be open to being "wrong" in order to learn. Your teaching evolves from day to day, from class to class and child to child. The more flexible you are, the more delightful the experience. And joy is what learning is about. This book should be something you enjoy; if it isn't, put it aside, give it away or use it for kindling. No need to make yourself crazy.

If you want to help your kids write stories that quiver with energy and compose poems that mysteriously express things that can't quite be put into words, you have to know what the process of writing is all about. You have to know the joy of the dance from within your own heart, or you can't hope to pass along any of the choreography.

Writing is a trip into the inner terrain; it involves the human spirit, the heart and soul. In order to teach writing, you must be a writer. In order to be a writer, you must write. In order to write, you must be open, seeking, and willing.

Fear and Loathing at the Typewriter Keys

I know. It's scary and hard. You have things you'd like to write about, but you don't know where to start and you don't know how to word it. And what if it isn't good and everybody laughs and you'll be embarrassed? There's too much to say, and you don't know how to compress it all into the right words, and you don't know how to put those words in the right order, and you're so confused about how to write a poem or a piece of fiction it freezes you on the spot. You are seized by a (nearly) irresistible urge to rearrange your sock drawer. You could color-coordinate it, or layer the socks in some kind of pleasing way that is a metaphor for contemporary urban life. Or you could make that Mississippi mud cake for your mate and kiddies; you haven't had a homemade dessert in eight months, and you are overwhelmed with sudden waves of guilt. Or you could sew a new dress.

Or you could sit down and write.

Face it; you can't deny it. You're a creative person. Cooking and cleaning are creative acts; hanging out with friends has an art and a style. Rearranging the furniture—ditto.

You know from your own experience that in order to teach something well, you have to understand it from the inside out. Your kids need you, and you are a devoted teacher who will do anything for their happiness and well-being. Therefore, you have to become a writer yourself. Don't panic; it's easy, it's enjoyable, it's satisfying. Just follow the steps.

Steps

Steps are how you get from place to place. A beautiful piece of choreography is built on steps performed with absolute commitment. Steps are how you get in the front door. The steps you will learn for writing are the same as those you will teach:

- Pictures speak louder than words. Compress a thousand words into a single evocative image.
- Specific verbs and nouns convey passion, life, and intensity. Don't walk if you want to ramble, hurl, trip, limp, shuffle, amble, twirl, leap, flop, tiptoe, tap, stomp, march, traipse, or stroll.
- We are living creatures. Living creatures, including writers and readers, know the world via their five senses. Use yours.

  ✎ Visions are things of the spirit, and writing springs out of having visions. Writing is a spiritual activity. Allow yourself rich, fanciful, and indulgent spiritual experiences. Get in the habit of loving your visions, whatever they may be. Your visions are not silly, immoral, vapid, melodramatic, or boring. Find yours through meditation, long walks, excessive daydreaming, doodling, bubblebaths, or whatever you like. Playfully and seriously seek them out, love them, and respect them.

Becoming the Writer You Are

Immerse yourself in pleasure.

No kidding, it helps to spoil yourself rotten. Buy a gorgeous notebook, or really indulge and get a computer if you can. Pens are sensual; find some you like. Perfume the air when you write, however you want to—incense, candles, tea, coffee, cigars, flowers, whatever. It's worth it. Writing is one of the most important and rewarding habits you can develop in your life.

Read like a mad creature, especially books about writing. I highly recommend Natalie Goldberg's *Writing Down the Bones* and many of the titles offered by Teachers & Writers Collaborative.

But read other stuff too. Short stories, novels, poems. Don't think about what is "good" or "bad" according to other people; develop your own taste. Some writing *is* good; it has integrity, it has depth and grace, it has the ability to horrify or move; magically, it means more than just the words on the page. So enjoy, devour it, be passionate about it for yourself.

Just as children learn gradually, so must you. Slowly you will begin to form ideas about style and taste. Slowly you will become graceful and adept at saying something in exactly the right way.

Write daily, anything at all. Don't concern yourself now with whether you want to write/should write/are writing a poem, a story, a play, a novel, or a quiet piece of personal history for yourself. What you are doing is writing . . . and writing and writing. Eventually, your voice will literally sing from the pages; eventually, things will find their own form. You will discover that you have written a poem or the opening (or middle or end or outline) to a story.

Daily Writing Activities

Journal

The journal is a collection of daily writings that give witness to your life. It can simply include details of events: who you saw, what you talked about, how green the mountains were, how much snow was predicted and how much you actually got. Journals are valuable for several reasons:

- They establish a daily rhythm of writing, a good habit that quickly becomes a healthy addiction.
- They encourage you to pay attention to the rich patterns and details of your life, things that often get forgotten or lost.
- They are histories and chronicles of the times.
- They provide an excellent source of material for later use.
- They remind you who you are, daily.

A journal doesn't have to be limited to the simple facts of your life and your aspirations. It can be a place to keep a running grocery list, or a bitch list—"Who I Hate Today and Why." You can jot down a change of address or a snatch of conversation you overheard. You can doodle and draw, or stick paint samples for safekeeping among the pages. It can get messy and spill with crossed-out words, or it can be neat and precise and calligraphied. It can certainly contain wild leaps of the imagination, outrageous lies, paranoid fantasies, grandiose dreams—anything at all. It is the texture of your life. If you haven't discovered it already, get a copy of Tristine Rainer's *The New Diary*. It's fabulous.

Stream of Consciousness

This can be included in your journal, or, if you prefer, you can keep a whole separate notebook for this type of writing. In stream-of-consciousness writing you are trying to put your ego to sleep. It is concerned with images, symbols, the rich undercurrent of the unfathomed self. Stream-of-consciousness writing has an utter lack of respect for logic, continuity, and sense. It means putting yourself into a kind of altered state in which you are very much in the moment. With practice, your hand and mind become attuned and you grow adept at grabbing each notion, picture, thought that floats through. For example:

Sun behind clouds. Dusty like shadows underneath. What? The trees, the sway and breeze, ducks wobble. Snap, crackle, pop. Pop and

Mom, popsicles. Orange pop at the corner Mom and Pop. Goes the weasel. But I can't anymore, Hear it, here it. Here it is. Here and now. The cow jumped over here over there over sun's sad face.

Because your ego isn't engaged, you aren't stopping yourself to impose a logical order over any of it. Stream of consciousness is total freedom; you are a baby's mind, free floating, grabbed by anything interesting, and you are simultaneously an adult's hand, writing quickly and effortlessly. When you are in this state you are functioning in absolute creativity. It is very close to a dream state, and it is very relaxing.

Automatic Writing

Automatic writing is an aspect of stream of consciousness which also involves tucking the interfering ego into bed so the creative mind and the hand can work in pure, uninterrupted tandem. Automatic writing is nothing more than a transcription of words and sounds babbling meaninglessly through your mind. Assonance, consonance, slant rhyme, and rhythm come forth in a curious and fascinating fashion when meaning is repressed.

Give yourself plenty of time to work your way into the heart of automatic writing. It is a type of verbal play that doesn't come easily; there is a strong tendency for ego interference. The conscious mind can search for a word or phrase to follow the previous words neatly, but the point is to learn to feel the sound, texture, rhythm, and physical taste of language automatically, naturally, and purely.

The best kind of order is not superimposed over chaos, but rises out of it. When the ego steps in and attempts to impose order over the effluvia of raw, meaningless sound, you don't have automatic writing. When the ego remains outside and allows your hand to capture the floating words and voices, the fractured sentences, the leftovers of conversation that are always buzzing in our minds whether we know it or not, you do have automatic writing.

You have been a speaking person for all of your life. Conversation, reading, listening, signposts, recipes, newspapers, eavesdropping, looking things up in the dictionary, television, and radio fill your days. Even your dreams—your nightly escapes—brim with language. You are so full of language that in some ways you are composed of it; it defines you. The more automatic writing you do, the more attuned your ear and your mind will be to the plastic material of language—its sounds, its cadence, its silences. When you go back over your writing later in the day, you will be surprised at what an artist your unconscious is. You will see all kinds of audio/rhythmic relationships, tensions, balances, and releases that you had no idea were happening.

In conversation, what is said is only part of the total message. In a piece of writing, what is said is also only a part. In conversation, a lifted eyebrow, a shrugged shoulder, the lighting of a cigarette all give clues as to what is meant. A statement can be delivered sarcastically or sentimentally without the words themselves changing. Because a piece of writing by its nature excludes the human being who authored it—as well as her raised eyebrow, her shrugged shoulder, her lit cigarette—it has to compensate in some other way. To be as forceful, passionate, and effective a message, it has to depend to a large degree on the physical sounds of its words. Daily or even weekly practice of automatic writing will help you to express exactly what you want in the most effective way when you are writing consciously.

Dreambook

There are two kinds of people in the world—those who discover dreambooks and are never the same, and those who couldn't care less. You have to try it to see if it's for you. If you are a person who dreams a lot, who dreams in color, whose dreams are ragged and wild, undecipherable, and fascinating, dreambooks are likely for you. If you are the kind of person who wants to be left alone with a morning cup of coffee and the stock-market reports, there's a good chance you won't be moved. If you like it when your son's girlfriend comes over and reads the tarot cards, if you like the paintings of any of the surrealists, and if the idea of sleeping with a Herkimer diamond crystal beneath your pillow on the off-chance it will make your dreams more vivid doesn't irritate you excessively, give dreambooks a throw.

Most people are interested in the symbols conjured by their deep, creative unconscious. We can't help it; we dream something, it affects us when we wake up, and we want to know—what does it *mean*? We feel as if a sacred truth will be revealed if we are smart enough to read the message. There are lots of theories about dreams. Some people believe that we all partake of a vast pool of archetypal images shared by all people of all cultures. If this is so, then your dreams *are* fathomable, even if mysterious. You believe some part of you is trying to tell you something in a way that is cosmic, and not idiosyncratic. That's what dream books you buy in a store are all about. For instance: *If you dream about a wooden-handled broom sweeping spaghetti that wiggles like headless snakes, it means you fear your lover's betrayal.*

Other people believe the symbols that abound in dreams are to a large degree personal and private. They have deep meaning to you, and are analyzable. Dreams, in this case, are a kind of language whose vocabulary and syntax come about because of experiences you have had in the past and what you've decided about them. Did you once fall out of an apple tree when you were seven while spying on your big sister kissing her boyfriend? Dreaming about apple pie could imply that you're repressing your romantic impulses in favor of security. Meaning abounds, but only you can find it.

Still other people believe that dreams are merely the leftover nervous impulses of the day, which trigger certain parts of the brain and stimulate images that occur higgledy-piggledy. To these people, dreams are meaningless, though sometimes amusing. In this case, anyone who goes searching for meaning in a dream is imposing over the (meaningless) series of dream images, a supra-dream logic or syntax that lends pseudo-meanings to the total dream. Personally, this seems to me to be kind of a killjoy attitude; I like to think of people as infinitely mysterious, with a subconscious, unconscious, id, and interior embossed with gold and glimmering with semi-precious stones. However, I admit I am to a small degree melodramatic. Perhaps dreams are nothing more than little electronic glitches. So what? They're still fun to write about.

Keeping a dreambook is merely a matter of jotting down parts and pieces of your nightly dreams. I knew a teenager who slept with her dreambook in one hand and her pen in the other. Before she was even awake each day, she would be writing. Only problem was, she often couldn't read what she had written down! You can keep your dreambook on tape, if you prefer, hitting the record button and babbling into the machine until the dream turns to phantasmagoria and evaporates. You might find that parts of your dream return to you during the day; go ahead and add in the new parts. Nothing says your dreambook has to be coherent, logical, or narrative. Draw in it, recollect parts of one dream and parts of another. You can even lie, if, as you write down the dream, your creative imagination takes over and rewrites it.

This will happen, I promise you: the more you attend to your dreams, the deeper, richer, more exciting and more satisfying your nightlife will become. It's a shock to realize that you are not simply the person you seem to be by day—the teacher, the parent, the shopper and cook—but that you really do occupy another world as well, a night world in which you have relationships and feelings just as you do by day. In some way, your dreams nourish you. If nothing else, they reawaken your interest in the daytime world, so that you can gather more material for the magic of your nightly constructions.

Memory Book

A memory book can be part of the journal, or you can keep it as a separate notebook. A memory book is pretty much just what it sounds like—a collection of recollections. You can arrange your memory book any way you want. There are two basic approaches, depending on how you like to order your life.

The first approach is to get a loose-leaf binder, one you like. They've got great ones out on the market now, at long last. You can get them in prints, or bright glossy yellow or red plastic. You can get them in hand-tooled leather. You can buy a big heavy blue one at Woolworth's and cover it with Contac paper, or velvet, or quilted squares. The loose-leaf notebook approach allows you to organize memories that arrive out of order. As a memory comes to you and you write it, you can simply insert it into the notebook in roughly chronological order.

Let's say your first entry was about when your grandmother died and you were seven and your grandfather made you kiss her good-bye and you were horrified. It goes in the notebook. Then the next day you remember the day you started your first job in high school, waiting on tables at a fast-food joint, stuck inside on what was probably the prettiest, sunniest day of the year. It goes in the notebook, after the first entry. Your third entry is about getting lost in the grocery store when you were about three. Put that one before your first entry. On the fourth day, you write about having a crush on your science teacher in sixth grade; that one gets wedged between your dead grandmother and waitressing. From the outside in, your life is put into temporal order.

You have other options if you use the loose-leaf approach. In fact, you can make copies of entries and keep several loose-leafs running at once, if you get really obsessed. Maybe you will want to organize your entries into sections.

Your sections could have to do with emotional states:

- **Elation**
- **Anxiety**
- **Fear of the Unknown**
- **Feeling trapped**

- **Contentment**

with themes you have recognized in your life:

- **Generosity**
- **Jealousy**
- **Self-effacement**
- **Curiosity**

with activities or events:

- **Parties**
- **Funerals**
- **School**
- **Sex**

or with any other organizing principle you think of. If you want, you can get fancy and color-code your entries.

If you like to write in pen, get one that really gives you a kick to use, and keep it with the notebook at all times. Don't let your mate use it, even to jot down a phone number. Too bad if your mate thinks you're being unreasonable. Memories are very private and personal things, and this pen is for the keeping of memories. Get lined paper, or even something luxurious, like a sheaf of handmade rag paper into which you can punch holes. If you compose at the keyboard, leave wide margins and punch holes in the paper after you have written.

The second approach is for those who like to take it as it comes. You don't want to put the entries in any kind of systematic arrangement. For you, the truth is in the memories being written in whatever order they arrive. Fine. Again, get a notebook and pen you like, or a stack of typing paper and something to stick the pages into as you finish with each.

Just to give yourself an idea of how many memories you have filling you up, and how rich and varied they are, take a piece of paper and divide it in half horizontally. Number each section one to ten. On the top half, quickly jot down ten events (these are not fully wrought memories, but simply a list) that occurred to you when you were eight. Some of them might be things you remember happening; some might be things you've heard about so many times from your family that you know they happened, although you yourself do not clearly remember; some of your list can be stuff that happens to all eight-year-old kids:

1. Almost drowned.
2. Kissed neighbor kid in the closet.

3. Found ten dollars in driveway.
4. Ran away; got as far as next town on bike.
5. Talked back to Grandma; got in trouble with Dad.
6. Moved; trouble adjusting to new school; didn't talk for three weeks.
7. Helped Uncle Gordon calve in the barn in the middle of the night.
8. Ice storm.
9. Began collecting fossils.
10. Lost at county fair.

Do the same with the bottom half of the paper, only now the memories will have to do with last year. You have just generated enough material for a solid month of writing five days a week! Memories, even more than dreams, respond well to attention. One memory seems to generate another. They sometimes come so quickly while you are writing that you can't capture them all. You start to feel as though you are the accumulation and culmination of everything you have ever passed through and everything that has ever passed through you. I suggest keeping several pages in the back of your notebook on which to jot down a running list of additional memories.

What you are going after with the memory book are the facts. Try to curb your impulses toward self (or other) analysis. Your memory book shouldn't be a forum for you to figure out exactly what went wrong and what you expected and what you didn't get. Nor should you allow a single entry to be a flowing, free-floating series of interconnected or unconnected moments in your life. Whereas the dreambook, automatic writing, and stream of consciousness allow and encourage quicksilver leaps of unbridled imagination and strive for pure, uncontrolled, and undisciplined creativity, the memory book seeks in each of its entries a sense of balance and form, a totality, and a feeling of closure by the entry's end. Each piece of writing that is entered in the memory book is framed by a single event involving certain people—period. Here are some guidelines:

- ❧ Focus on a single event, not a series. Write about getting lost in the woods, not about getting lost and then getting in trouble later.

- ❧ Write about a brief, easily contained block of time. The most intense memories are concentrated; they are about occurrences so sharp and quick that they literally became inscribed in your brain cells.

❧ Focus primarily on sensory detail. This is one of the most important tenets of good writing, and I will return to it again and again. We are in truth connected to the world and to one another through our bodies. Our bodies know what they know through our senses. Smells are the most memorable. A whiff of perfume can bring back the full memory of someone you haven't seen in fifteen years more quickly than a photograph. Consider your memory in terms of smells, textures, temperatures, sounds, tastes, visual details; color, size, and shape.

❧ Feel free to experiment. Go the next step. Add details you know weren't there, change the characters if you wish. Change the ending if you wish. You are still writing about the truth on some level; you are writing about the truth of your feelings.

❧ Do not editorialize. You are writing about what happened, not about what you think about it now from the vantage point of the present.

❧ Try writing in the present tense. It will help make the memory sing again; it will make it immediate and palpable.

❧ Pay attention to how you describe activity, movement, motion. Did your teacher in fact *waddle*? Picture it in your mind's eye. Allow yourself to be wordless for a moment and try out meaningless sounds. Grunt and murmur. Use a thesaurus or another reference tool to seek out just the right verb.

❧ Be as specific as possible about all details. The right word, be it noun or verb, is so much more effective than an endless string of modifiers.

❧ Avoid words of judgement: *beautiful, nice, fun, pretty, mean, bad* are imageless and vague.

Meditation and Writing

I was in a school that was just this side of torture. There were serious disagreements about the nature of education between school board and principal, between principal and teachers. Each classroom was a sad world unto itself. The teachers felt unappreciated because they were. The more exhausted among them had begun to question their own worth. The kids dragged themselves through the halls and picked fights, outraged over a miscast glance. Misery.

It was late in the school year and the sixth grade was in full force, practicing curled lips and cool, despising glances for next year at the big school. In class, they wrote, sort of. But their hearts weren't in it, and it showed.

On the sixth and final day of my ALPS poetry residency, I walked into the classroom to find it in full, screaming chaos. Kids were everywhere, leaning out windows to shout at passersby, curled up in corners gossiping, crouched in hand-to-hand combat position between the rows of desks.

I looked around. No teacher. I looked again. Behind several stacks of books and flocks of test papers, a substitute sat, lost in a book whose pages she turned with a licked finger.

I blew up. I don't remember what I said, but very quickly the kids were sitting at their desks. Probably I threatened them with the principal; an idle threat to say the least: I was as afraid of him as they were. The spitballs and comments continued to fly, and in a rage, I snapped out the lights and ordered them to put down their heads. I was shocked when they did so. In the first moments of silence that followed, I panicked. The moment they sat up, pandemonium was sure to break out. The substitute continued to read, even in the half-darkened room. She made me so mad I went to the windows and let down the blinds. I looked at my hands and was surprised to see them shaking.

"Just take a quiet, deep breath. I want you to get calm," I said to myself out loud. Immediately I was mortified. But a deep, sweet sigh rippled through the darkness. They thought I was talking to them.

"Again," I said, and again they breathed deeply.

"Whatever it is you're thinking about, stop. If you're worrying about a test, stop. If you're thinking about someone you like, stop. If you're thinking about what you're going to do after school, stop. Just stop thinking. Your mind is empty."

They breathed in unison. I began to panic again. It occurred to me that I better plant something in their minds for them to focus on.

"You are in the basement of a building you've never been in before," I said. I'm not sure where the idea came from; perhaps it was because I had just bought a house and was scared to go down the rickety basement stairs.

"Look at the floors. What are they made of? Get down on your knees inside your mind and really look." They continued to breathe deeply, as if in sleep; but they were awake, focused, concentrating.

"Look around the room, gather as many details as you can. What do you smell, and where is it coming from? What is the source of light? Look at it, look hard. Suddenly something happens!"

Their bodies tensed. One girl gasped.

"What? Where did it happen, and what do you do now, where do you go?"

I asked them many more questions—location, time, quality of light, atmosphere, what they could feel with their hands, and so on. Together we went from the basement, up the stairs, to the first floor, then still higher into the attic.

I didn't know where it was going to go; I didn't even know I was finished talking until I realized I had fallen silent for a few moments. I told them to breathe again, deeply. When I switched on the lights, they grabbed paper and began to write wildly. They wrote pages and pages, their handwriting jagged, crazy, energized. They didn't stop to analyze what they were writing about, they didn't stop to edit what they were writing, they didn't try to explain anything. They just wrote. They had had visions, and out of the visions came the power to write.

I moved around the room, glancing over their shoulders. I was thrilled to discover that some kids were writing absolutely realistic and deeply evocative pieces, while others worked on stories that were surreal. Some writers lingered with their language, considering a twist of phrase or a particularly strong image, while others were compelled forth along a strong and dramatic narrative line. Each writer's work was different; each had a voice that was authentic and unique.

After a long time, they were finished. There were none of the usual questions: How long does it have to be? Should I print or write? Can I use a pen? They wrote what needed to be said, and they were finished when the need was satisfied. We only had a couple of minutes before my time was up. I started to gather my books together, but they stopped me. They wanted to talk about what had just happened.

"Did we get hypnotized?" whispered a girl in the back. Normally she was hell on wheels.

Good lord. *Did* they? If so, I was most certainly in big trouble. You just can't go around hypnotizing kids, at least not without a written permission slip from their parents. I started to stammer, and was thankfully interrupted.

"No, stupid," snarled a boy I knew for a fact had a mad crush on the girl. "She didn't tell us what to do."

"She told us what to see!" Someone yelled out.

"She didn't," the boy patiently explained. "She told us 'What did we see?' She told us use your own brains, dummies."

I stood there with my mouth open. Sweetness and light! I was not only saved from the wrath of forty-six parents carrying pitchforks and lanterns, a towering principal leading the pack, and a possible jail term, I was being taught something very important, something I hadn't known before.

Teaching is about telling your students to use their own brains.

The meditation is useful in several ways:

- It allows a transition from the exterior to the interior world. The interior world becomes bigger and more important. The deep breathing calms anxieties over writing and helps the writer focus on the vision instead of on distractions.

- It provides the writer with material via the developing vision. After meditation, writers are completely prepared to begin writing.

- It compels. Vivid images arrived at through meditation attain a sort of vibrancy that hurl the writer into an urgent desire to write.

- It allows the imagination a forum, while grounding the images that rise in the writer's mind via prompt questions.

- It allows a separation between the social world and the personal world. Children who lift their heads and open their eyes after meditation are very focused on themselves and no longer on the community of the classroom.

There are two things to remember when using this technique in the classroom:

1. Your voice is your tool. Pitch it to soothe and to excite; bring it high and low; play it like music.
2. Your questions are solely prompts to your kids' imaginations. They must be very general and open to interpretation, yet grounded in sensory perception and fact (e.g. Where are you exactly? What sounds do you hear? What direction are they coming from? What is making them? How do you feel in your body? What happens next?).

It may take you a while to become comfortable with this technique in the classroom. Play with your voice and with your pacing, and don't be discouraged. Use it alone too. Close your eyes and breathe slowly and deeply. Silently ask yourself questions to discover what it is you are about to write, to suggest a rough idea that your visioning mind will then flesh out.

Workshops and Classes

Almost every community offers a course in creative writing through a local university, community college, high school, or YMCA. There are always many levels of experience represented in them, so it doesn't matter if you are a rote beginner or if you have been writing in secret under your bed at midnight for the last seven years. It's time to find others like yourself and rub noses.

Workshops can be run in different ways. Some instructors prefer to discuss student writing sequentially, to insure that everyone gets a fair shake of attention. Other instructors leave it up to the class; if someone writes twice as much, they may get their work discussed twice as much.

Many teachers set aside a block of time each session for in-class writing. Often, the writing follows a discussion and is to a greater or lesser degree, assigned. After the writing time the writers might share work in a large group or in several small ones.

Some instructors will give you individual or group assignments for the following week. Get in the habit of being disciplined about writing. It's good for you.

On the off-chance you live in an area that doesn't offer a class, you can organize your own writing workshop. Keep it small. You might want to start with yourself and three or four other teachers or friends. You might want to assign a group leader each week for the first month. Here are some basic guidelines for smooth, useful workshops:

> ❧ **Bring one clean, readable, double-spaced copy for each reader. Some people like to write comments in the margins; others are driven mad by this behavior. Don't bring in handwritten copies. Hire a typist if necessary.**

> ❧ **When it is your turn to be critiqued, do not verbally respond. Jot down comments as they come in. If you want to discuss one later, put a star next to it. Don't let your ego inflate at compliments; don't let yourself go to pieces over criticism.**

> ❧ **Your critique of others' work must be sincere and it must be honest. Be specific. Praise what is praiseworthy, and address what needs work. But remember to be kind. The last thing you want is to discourage this person.**

- ✎ Remember that another person's work is not your vision; you do not have permission to rewrite the story for the author.

- ✎ Keep all pieces of writing and all comments about them together someplace safe. Don't rewrite anything you don't want to. Do rewrite anything you feel charged up about. Periodically go through the work and see if anything now turns you on that you weren't interested in redoing before. As your technique and tools increase, so will your visions.

Summary

The more writing you do, the more attuned to the power of words you will become. Whether you decide to explore journals, memory books, dreambooks, stream of consciousness, automatic writing, poetry, fiction, plays, travelogues, or even letter writing, there are a few very basic things to keep in mind:

- ✎ Always go for the exact word. Strong verbs and precise nouns still have the magic of image in them. Weak, overused verbs and nonprecise nouns have had their images worn out by overuse. Your writing has only as much power as the image it creates in the reader's mind.

- ✎ Focus on sensory perceptions. Your writing will seize the reader by the throat if it keeps her body busy. Mention of scents, sounds, textures are evocative, and call out for the readers' full participation in the writing's unfolding.

- ✎ Avoid, at all costs, simple, imageless value judgements. Certain words, usually adjectives, are used so frequently that they mean almost nothing at all; they force upon the reader only a vague sense of how she is expected to feel about a character or situation. Strong writing does not force a reader toward any conclusions; strong writing allows and encourages a reader to arrive at certain conclusions based on the facts, details, and orchestration of the writing. Try not to use: beautiful, ugly, pretty, mean, nice, friendly, fun, funny, good, bad.

- ✎ Literally see images of what you are writing, and capture the spirits of the images. Writing is an abstraction of speaking. Whereas speech includes gestures, pregnant pauses, and all kinds of other unspoken messages, writing, by its nature, cannot. It must in some way compensate. Writing does not imitate speaking; it gives the illusion of speaking. Speaking is in effect three-dimensional; writing is flat. If it is good, its effect is to spring into vivid, three-dimensional life in the mind of the reader. This cannot possibly happen if the writer, during the making of writing, does not in truth see before her eyes the images projected by her mind.

2

Kindergarten: Brilliant Innocence

From the Mouths of Babes

Once, a long time ago, when your grandparents' parents were children, fish had feet. Some fish had 4 feet, some fish had 5 feet, some fish had 6 feet, no fish had 7 feet, and some fish had 8 feet. The fish wore yellow, orange, and blue shoes made out of scales. When they walked they sounded like this: *tick-tick-tick.* They sounded like clocks. But there was a problem. There was one fish who did not wear yellow, orange, and blue shoes made out of scales. His feet were different. His feet were round. His shoes were like a horse's shoes. When he walked, he sounded like a brontosaurus walking. When he walked, he sounded like thunder. When he walked, the other fish got bounced up in the air and down again, up and down, and this made them angry. They wouldn't play with the brontosaurus fish, or talk to him. The brontosaurus fish became very sad. He was so sad he couldn't move, he couldn't even walk. He was afraid to walk because if he did, the other fish would bounce up into the air and down onto the ground, up and down. So he just stood there, and cried and cried. Then when he was done crying, he looked at the sky that was as blue as a bluebird. He didn't see the bluebird that flew out of the sky to talk to him, because the bluebird was as blue as the sky, and they looked alike. The bluebird said, "Don't cry, I will take you with me into the sky." So the fish flapped his feet and together they flew into the sky. The fish met the hawk, the robin redbreast, the owl, the sun, all the clouds, and the wind, and all of them said "You are not a fish at all, you belong in the sky with us." So the brontosaurus fish, who wasn't a fish after all, flapped his feet and stayed in the sky forever.

—*Chloe Dresser's preschool class*

The above story was created by a group of preschool storytellers, the result of my first creative "writing" workshop with very young children. My friend Chloe had repeatedly invited me to visit her preschool class and "do your creative writing thing with them." I put her off, avoided her for weeks, said I'd think about it, and finally, with a great deal of trepidation, agreed. The kids, she told me, were four and five. There were twenty-two of them, and they were used to working in a big circle, as a group.

Panic. I had worked with first graders at the end of the school year on occasion, but preschool?

On the one hand, I told myself to give it a throw. If it doesn't work it doesn't work, big deal, who cares. Might even learn something.

On the other hand, a dark, guttural, and slightly paranoid voice deep in the back of my head growled twice and snarled, "Ha! You've told Chloe 732 times about the stories and poems your students write. If you fail with her kids, she'll think you're a crummy teacher and she'll tell her husband, your mutual six closest friends, and the mailman, who will spread it all over town along with other incidental gossip. What kind of fool would leave herself open to such ridicule?"

Me.

Before going to her class, in order to decide upon the best course of action, I considered the information I had at hand about preschoolers:

> Preschoolers have a short attention span.
> Some preschoolers are bossy and take over.
> Some preschoolers are shy and won't look at you.
> Preschoolers will surprise you by what they say.
> Preschoolers like to ask and answer questions.

I decided working in a big circle was the best plan. They were used to circles and knew how to follow circle rules. In a circle:

> I would immediately sense when their group attention
> span was flagging.
> Everyone would have the satisfaction of having created
> the story.
> Bossy kids couldn't take over.
> Shy kids wouldn't be pressured to speak, but would still

feel themselves part of the creative group.
Their surprising and creative ideas would provide the
story's essence.
I could exploit their natural curiosity and authority in the
crafting of a story.

More on the making of this story later.

Architects of the Imagination

Everyone, whether adult or child, professional writer or nonwriter,
teacher or parent, is governed by two different truths. The first is the truth
of world experience. This is the shared world we collectively create,
recognize, and occupy. It's the stuff everybody knows: red light means
stop; dogs don't fly; fish don't walk; nighttime is for sleeping; if you don't
brush your teeth you lose them and then nobody will be able to understand you when you talk.

The second is the private truth of the interior; the truth of feelings. This
is the land of fantasy, magic and dreams, rich with symbol, color, music,
and mystery. In the interior, some of the shared truths don't stand up
anymore; fish might walk or red lights might not stop anybody. In the
inner world, external rules are challenged, and their destruction can
produce fear or excitement or pure absurd silliness when everything
looks and acts like a cartoon.

Children are natural editors. A story that begins in the realm of magic
stays there, unwrapping its glittering details and impossible narrative in
midair from beginning to end. If anyone tries to bring it to the level of the
mundane, there is a general outcry. A tale that begins in the world of
everyday but quickly leaps into a magical dimension will usually in fact
be a carefully balanced story within a story. It will present a false front of
reality concealing a bizarre, unreal world that we glimpse through a rent
in the fabric. Children, those architects of imagination, will finish this type
of story off with a return at the story's end to the shared world in which
it began.

In addition to being natural editors, children are both careful historians
and creative storytellers. Sometimes stories are pretty much about the
way it is; five-year-olds are still so fresh and sweetly attuned to the world
that reality is just as amazing and delightful as dream, indeed, often more
so.

A pre-primary teacher told me her children were unclear about the difference between the world of so-called "reality" and that of make-believe. She wanted me to do a lesson in which I urged the young writers to ground their work in reality. The class and I had a nice, long talk about sounds, narrowed it down to morning sounds, categorized morning sounds into those made by machines (cars, toasters, coffee drippers, etc.), those made by animals (birds flapping, mewling kittens, puppies slurping water), and those made by humans (mommy's shoes making footsteps, yawning, the sound of your own heartbeat under the blankets). After the group discussion, the kids returned to their tables to draw and write about what they heard that morning.

One boy wrote, "a lin grlng" (a lion growling). Teacher called me over and pointed meaningfully. Although I kind of liked the idea of waking up to hear a lion growling, I understood that she was concerned about "reality." I bent over and read his words out loud. He glowed with pride. I congratulated him. He nodded. I took a deep breath, and said in my most therapeutic voice, "And what was it really—Was it really a machine you heard, that sounded like a growling lion?" He shook his head and knitted his eyebrows. "Was it really your pet that was growling?" He glared at me with the look of one betrayed. "Was it really inside your head that you heard the growling lion?"

"No, it was *really* a lion," he said at last, unable to tolerate any more of what was clearly my mistake. All week I'd been encouraging him to believe in his own perceptions, and now here I was telling him not to!

"Tell me where the lion was," I quickly asked, thinking that might provide a clue.

"Inside the TV," he said solemnly, "and when my mommy turned it off, I heard eggs cackling in the frying pan!"

Story Circles and the Pre-Literate "Writer"

Once in a while I find a teacher who feels that there is little point in bringing a creative writing program to her kindergarten class. "My kids don't know how to write," she will say nervously, as if it is her own failure.

Writing is merely a convenience and a convention for its users; it isn't the essence of language. As any good or even mediocre anthropologist will be quick to point out, cultures that lack "writing" offer nonetheless a rich and various story-making tradition. Oral tales that explain natural or supernatural phenomena, instruct morally, or preserve the history of the people through narrative are found in all cultures.

I look at kindergartners the way an anthropologist looks at a primitive tribe—with fascination, awe, and more than a little envy. Without the guidance/interference of an adult, kindergartners will make up stories to explain the baffling questions that occur at age five. Their stories are dramatic and eventful, rich and symbolic.

Just as a tribal culture will ritualize the telling of an already-familiar tale by gathering the group together around a fire, kindergartners like to ritualize the act of telling in a story circle. Story circles are great. Because they're round, no one feels left out. In a circle, it's much easier to address lots of faces at once without straining—both for the teacher and the children. The story circle has its own cultural mores to which most five-year-olds subscribe. Don't talk when somebody else is, because it's distracting. Don't get up and walk around because everyone will look at you and tell you to sit down. Anyone can contribute. Silence is nice, too; we don't have to talk all the time. And when you feel safe in the community of your friends, it's easy to feel good about yourself and to think creatively.

It's a good idea to encourage the kids to establish their own rules for the story circle. They know themselves and each other pretty well and will set limits they know they need. Besides, they will be a lot more likely to remember and adhere to guidelines that they establish themselves. Some classes emphasize not talking when someone else has the floor; other classes have more of a problem with people getting up and walking around.

I think the best moment of my entire life came when a thoughtful, curly-topped little redhead girl with perfectly bowed lips and a freckled nose politely raised her hand to contribute a rule. I called on her, she batted her lashes, sucked most of the air out of the room and into her lungs, and bellowed, "NEVER STICK UP YOUR MIDDLE FINGER AT ANYBODY!!!" Her teacher and I managed to regain our composure after we had fallen sideways off our chairs guffawing hysterically. I pointed out that this was a good rule for life, but now we were looking for special rules just for the story circle. They got it, offered the usual raise-your-hand-to-talk suggestions, and we carried on.

Asking Questions

By nature, group stories are organic. They have a lively spirit. A group story is created by the tribe working together, but it's more than the sum total of the ideas and energy the individuals put into it. It's synergistic.

The story circle is composed of one leader and any number of kids. The leader has a primary role—to stimulate ideas through a series of directive questions; and a secondary role—to maintain an intense, concentrated group focus.

Your questions must be extremely spare. They are prompts only. If the question is rejected by the group, let it go. Just as the story itself is organic, growing naturally piece by piece, your prompt questions must be organic—what you sincerely want to know. If several children have several possible answers to a prompt question, listen carefully to each one. Sometimes a story is so hot and the group is so involved with its making that everyone has a zillion different ideas. Select carefully; each answer that you pick to stitch into the fabric of the story both deepens the story's overall pattern and leads toward the next event.

The questions you ask serve one of two purposes:

1. They move the story forward through time on a narrative track, involving cause and effect, surprise twists, or some other event. These questions are in the nature of "And then what happened?"

2. They channel the story into deeper, richer territory by asking for details of setting, character, or mood. These questions stop the story's temporal, logical movement and freeze all action in space while the group considers the finer points:

   Why was the mother angry at the monster?
   What kind of shoes did the kangaroo wear?
   What did the boy's treehouse look like?

It is essential that you, as leader, be open and ignorant. Begin with an opening idea, character, or setting. Nothing more. Don't offer a character in a place doing something; already they will realize it isn't their story but yours. And allow yourself to be pleasantly surprised rather than annoyed if the group refuses your opening in favor of one of their own making. Grab it. You can always use yours another day.

I used to know a teeny tiny little girl. Do you know where she lived?

This possible opening offers a unique character to the children and also assumes that you share a collective body of knowledge, even if it is made up as you go along. The teeny tiny girl might suggest to one group a Thumbellina, a magical character who obviously lives in a fairy-tale world. To another group, the teeny tiny girl might simply be young or small for her age, a situation that becomes the basis for the story's problem.

Each question requires only one answer. If several kids have great ideas, listen to them and choose one quickly. Don't feel you have to go around the circle asking for twenty-two different answers to each question. Nothing will get made that way, and everyone will get bored and cranky, including you.

And remember, you are a member of the group, too. There will be times when you have an idea too fun to pass by. I was working with a second-grade class in New Berlin who were making up a ghost story. The ghost went to school in a kid's pocket, flew around, caused trouble, flew into the teacher's pocket. "And then what happened?" I asked.

"I sneezed," came the answer, from the mouth of the class's real teacher, "and I thought the ghost was my hankie, and so I wadded him up and blew my nose!"

The kids loved it, I loved it, and the teacher looked quite pleased with her wonderful idea. In addition, her answer subtly touched the interface between the invented, fictional world of make-believe and the actual, physical world of shared experience. She became simultaneously the real teacher, and the teacher in the story. This transformation by extension allowed each child in her classroom to be simultaneously maker of the tale, and character within it. Who says you can't be in two places at once?

Caution

Beware of leading too much with your questions. "Did" questions are absolutely out. They have only two answers—yes and no. And they don't do a thing to prompt the children's own creative thinking. The kids will either want to please you by assuring you that yes, the flower did go to school or they will tease you by rejecting your obviously loaded suggestion. Ask:

- why
- how
- where
- who
- what

Rephrase the prompt question: How did the flower learn to read? Sure, "at school" is the most likely answer, but the question phrased in this way allows for a surprising spontaneous eruption of unique ideas. Maybe the flower taught herself. How? By reading the backs of cereal boxes.

By slowing things down, examining the story for its real substance, you will help your children realize that good literature, whether it is in the oral tradition or written in a book, offers solid detail for the listener/reader to grab hold of and smell and taste and pet. It makes the story yummy.

Analyzing the Process

The best way to explain how the story of the brontosaurus fish came about will be to transcribe the questions I asked and the answers the kids gave. Notice that after each accepted answer I repeated the story back to them, incorporating the new information into the growing body of the story.

Teacher: Once, a long time ago, when your grandparents' parents were children, fish had feet. What kind of feet did they have?

Students: Four!
Five!
Six!
[pause, grins]
Eight!

Teacher: No fish had seven feet?

Student: Nope. How would they walk?

Teacher: *Once, a long time ago, when your grandparents' parents were children, fish had feet. Some fish had 4 feet, some fish had 5 feet, some fish had 6 feet, no fish had 7 feet, and some fish had 8 feet.* What did these fishes wear?

Student: Shoes, silly.

Teacher: Right, shoes. What kind?

Students: Colors.
Yellow ones.
Blue ones because of the ocean that fishes like.
Orange.

Teacher: They like colors. I never saw blue, yellow, and orange shoes for fishes. What were they made out of?

Students: Scales.
And when they walked, they sounded *tick-tick*.

Teacher: I've heard that sound before. What else goes *tick-tick*?

Students: Clock.
Yup. Sounds like clocks. And them too.

Teacher: [checking] The fish sounded like clocks?

Student: Yeah, when they walked. *tick-tick*. [giggles]

Teacher: Ok.
Once, a long time ago, when your grandparents' parents were children, fish had feet. Some fish had 4 feet, some fish had 5 feet, some fish had 6 feet, no fish had 7 feet and some fish had 8 feet. The fish wore yellow, orange, and blue shoes made out of scales. When they walked they sounded like this: tick-tick-tick. They sounded like clocks.

Teacher: But! [dramatic pause; I gasp; they gasp] But!

Student: One didn't.

Teacher: Huh? One what? Didn't what?

Student: One fish didn't wear those shoes. Those scales on his feet. [long silence; thinking]

Teacher: Why?

Students: Different kinds of feet.
Round ones.

Teacher: Hmmm. Fish with round feet. Hmmmm.

Students: Oh! Hey, listen to me! They were round like a horse foot.
No, they were round like something else; it's my answer.
No, they were! He wore horse's shoes and when he walked he sounded like a brontosaurus walking.
When he walked, he sounded like thunder!

Teacher: Wow. What happened when he walked?

Students: [long pause] Nothing.
I don't know.
My mommy picks me up after school every day.
Shutup, stupid. [long pause]

Teacher: Close your eyes. Can you see the round-footed fish who walks like a big, heavy brontosaurus? He sounds like thunder.
Boooomm! Boooommm!

Student:	*Boooooom!* Gaaaa! I'm getting bounced in the air. And falling down again.
Teacher:	*When he walked, the other fish got bounced up in the air and down again, up and down, and this made them, made them . . .*
Students:	Furious. Angry. *Grrrrrr.* They said go away, we won't play.
Teacher:	[long face; sigh; I move to the middle of the circle and stand uncertainly] And he was so sad he . . .
Students:	Couldn't even walk. Cause if he walked, boy oh boy. Up and down again. He cried. Just stood there and looked up at the sky.
Teacher:	*The brontosaurus fish became very sad. He was so sad he couldn't move, he couldn't even walk. He was afraid to walk because if he did, the other fish would bounce up into the air and down onto the ground, up and down. So he just stood there, and cried. Then when he was done crying, he looked at the sky.* [I stop to catch my breath]
Students:	Blue sky. Bluebird sky. [giggles]
Teacher:	*Looked at the sky that was as blue as a bluebird.*
Student:	Then a bluebird did come.
Teacher:	How blue was the bluebird?
Students:	Blue. A bird. Blue. The sky is blue and the bluebird too, same thing. Oh! [*frantic waving of arms; kid is so excited she topples over*] The blue sky has the bluebird inside but you, I mean the fish, doesn't see the bluebird right away because it . . . it . . . Disappears inside the blue. Right. What's the word? Paint does it.
Teacher:	Blends in?
Student:	Yeah.
Teacher:	*Then when he was done crying, he looked at the sky that was as blue as a bluebird. He didn't see the bluebird that flew out of the sky to talk to him, because the bluebird was as blue as the sky and they looked alike.*

	Yes? Next? You're doing great.
Students:	Bird talks.
	Ohhhhhh, don't cry. I'll take you up.
Teacher:	How?
Student:	Flapped his feet.
Teacher:	*The bluebird said, don't cry, I will take you with me into the sky. So the fish flapped his feet and together they flew into the sky.*
Students:	You know what? I saw a hawk once.
	I saw a owl.
	I saw a robin reddress.
Teacher:	Who else lives in the sky?
Students:	Sun.
	Windy windy windy.
	Cotton clouds.
	White clouds.
	Toilet paper. [nasty, delighted giggles]
Teacher:	*The fish met the hawk, the robin redbreast, the owl, the sun, all the clouds, and the wind, and all of them . . . .*
Students:	I'm hungry.
	Said hi!
Teacher:	Hi? That's it? Hi and bye?
Students:	Hi! Wanna live with me?
	Hey! You're a fish.
	Hey! You're not a fish. More like a bird.
Teacher:	*said, you are not a fish at all, you belong in the sky with us. So the brontosaurus fish, who wasn't a fish at all, flapped his feet and stayed in the sky forever.*

Kindergartners naturally speak in snatches of phrase or single words. Story circles have a focused, intense energy to them, and you'll find as you work with your group that they sometimes begin a statement only to drop back and let someone else finish it. Keep track of what's happening in the group to be sure that no one is getting shouted down or bullied, but don't coax a child who has begun a statement and then loses the energy for it or can't find a word. Everyone will be there as much as they can be; accept it and love them for it. The story made by a group is a lot like a crazy quilt; you add things as you come upon them in the sewing box.

Stop frequently and repeat the information to them. They may make you go back to an earlier point in the story and change it. Remember that they are in charge; you are just the secretary. You have to make the jump for them sometimes ("I'm getting bounced up in the air!"—the speaker here isn't a kid anymore, she's a footed fish, and she assumes I know it). If you aren't sure you understood something that was said, ask again. Beware of interpreting too much. You are there only to act as the speaker out of whose mouth come the ideas from the group-brain. You cannot take over, only repeat.

Extratextual Babble

With kids this young, and sometimes with older kids, you may get two kinds of statements that have nothing to do with the story. One is a report of how they are doing— "I'm hungry"; "Shutup stupid"—and the other is a piece of information that has absolutely nothing to do with anything happening in the group text ("My mommy picks me up every day after school"). This isn't necessarily an indication of boredom. Literature, whether oral or written, doesn't have a unique material in which it occurs. This is really an interesting problem. Painters create using paint, dancers create using the body's movements through space, musicians (those blessed creatures) use silence, rhythm, and sound. Writers, poor cousins, haven't got a material that isn't already being used almost constantly by themselves and everyone else to communicate everything from a whim to an annoyance. This is really confusing for kids. They know the words in the story circle are for the circle, but how else do they let you know they have a physical need? The moments of befuddlement that lead to extratextual information ("My mommy picks me up . . . ") are one of two things. The child is either feeling outside the group and signals this with a verbal contribution that isn't even close, or the child has momentarily fallen through a slight rip in the cosmos. It isn't necessary to address these comments. Gently repeat the question. If, however, the kid doesn't catch your drift and tries to begin an animated conversation with you that (1) has nothing to do with the work in progress and (2) effectively excludes the other members of the group, stop him mid-word with "We are working on the story now. You can tell me later." Then immediately turn back to the group and repeat the prompt question.

Of course, some kids are strong-willed. A while back I was in a story circle that contained an extremely bright, creative youngster. She had managed to wedge herself into an almost nonexistent spot next to me. Her hand was the first one to shoot up, even before the prompt question had left my mouth. Sometimes she didn't even wait for me to finish talking before she began to supply the next idea—without raised hand. I reminded her several times that she was talking without giving other people a chance. This gentle reprimand didn't phase her in the slightest.

"Yes," she responded, "but I want to talk!"

Finally, I rather pointedly shifted my weight so that my back was firmly presented to her. After a moment, she compensated for my apparent rudeness by reaching around as well as she was able to madly wave her hand in the periphery of my vision. When that didn't work, I heard her clear her throat. I ignored her. Her counterattack consisted of several taps on my shoulder, accompanied by almost violent throat clearing. I was enjoying this nonverbal and absolutely clear communication up to but not including the moment in which she firmly grabbed one of my braids and gave it a sharp pull!

Strut Your Style

While I caution you against too much teacherly interference in the making of the story, I do not want to inhibit you as a stylist. You are receiving answers, on a good day, from your entire class. These answers will be choppy—single words sometimes, partial phrases sometimes. What you are seeking from the children are ideas, glimmers of creation. Your job, in addition to editing (i.e., choosing what goes in, what stays out) and prompting, is to provide the linguistic texture of the story. You provide the voice of the storyteller. You phrase ideas and link them together, repeat phrases, draw out a section of the story, or couch it in a particular cadence. The way you do this will be the difference between a story that is stuffed with potential (from their great ideas) but fails due to incomplete execution, and one whose potential is realized.

The Power That Comes from Within

Children learn to read after they have become comfortable with writing. If you think about it, it makes sense: the first reader had to postdate the first writer—either that, or take upon herself the task of scribing out some primitive lines and figures on the cave wall so that she would have something to read!

Both reading and writing are pure and utter magic; as adults, we have learned to forget this fact, or we would constantly be in a state of spiritual ecstasy and never get anything done. Writing is a completely silent way of talking; not only that, it's a completely silent way of talking in the future. You write something down, then you let people hear your words without even being there to move your mouth. Tomorrow they can read it and know your mind again. And if you forget what you were thinking about, you can read your own words and remember.

Nothing is more moving than being near a kid who is grasping the power and magic and spiritual heart of writing for the first time. I'd been working with Mrs. Conlee's class for two weeks. Each day, they threw themselves into telling a group story and then took off to their tables to capture the spirits of the stories in drawings and, for some, in letters. On this particular day, the group created the following story:

> Once there was a boy who dreamed he could fly. He wanted to fly so much that he turned into a bird. The way he did it was to make himself wings out of sticks and feathers. He tied the sticks and feathers to his arms and went to a mountainside and jumped off. He decided he would fly to Florida to visit his aunt, because winter was coming. He jumped up and flapped his wings, and he turned into a real bird. He flew and flew, but then he felt cold on his back and it was Winter, flying faster than him. Winter got on top of him and no matter how fast he flew, he couldn't get away. Winter froze him into a big solid block of ice. He was stuck, and he was very sad and began to miss his mother and father and his sister. He waited for the ice to melt but the sun wasn't warm enough to melt it. He turned back into a boy with sticks and feathers for wings, and he used the pointed tip of his stick to break the ice until he could get out. He got out and began to fly again, and again Winter got him. This time he got snowed on and his wings became heavier and heavier with snow, until he couldn't flap them anymore. The snow covered him all over and weighed him down, lower and lower. Finally, he floated all the way down to the ground, and he turned into a boy again, and he took off his stick and feather wings, and he walked back to his home where his mother and father and sister were very glad to see him and kissed him a lot and tucked him into his bed.
>
> —*Mrs. Conlee's kindergarten, D. P. Sutherland School*

The whole class was actively involved in the story's creation. They liked the major struggle of wills going on here. A boy who wishes to fly so much that he magically becomes a bird by use of a talisman (stick and feathers) comes up against the even greater power of nature (the coming of winter). This greater power stops the bird/boy who has defied certain natural laws, by freezing him into a block of ice. But (catch this, it's beautiful) the boy cleverly uses the talisman as a tool to dig out of the ice and once again defies nature. Winter's revenge—covering the boy/bird's wings with snow—shows a simultaneous acceptance of the boy's transformation outside the laws of nature. Ultimately, of course, nature wins: the snow is simply too heavy, and the bird/boy cannot flap his wings anymore. Nature's victory is sweet more than bitter: because of it, the boy is returned to the loving bosom of his family, richer for his experience, more confident for his new-found abilities, and, in short, empowered from within. If nature says he must be a boy and live with a family, well then he will, and he will be happy. Still, he knows that his imagination is so great that he can temporarily leap the bounds to soar into the sky and gain another perspective.

The entire class was excited. They leaned forward into the story circle, sliding toward me on their behinds until they were clustered around my knees and the teacher and I had to move them back into the circle. One little guy in particular was taken with the story. Michael had donated several wonderful images, including the one about making the wings from sticks and feathers, and the fact that the wings turned the boy into a real bird. His eyes shimmered as the tale unfolded.

While the other children chattered and babbled about the story on their way back to their desks, he quietly took the paper I offered and retreated to a back table that is kept by the teacher for silent work. Residents of the other five tables in the classroom bubbled joyfully, sounding out words, asking for help in remembering the shape of a particular letter. Michael bent over his work, breathing softly and murmuring to himself as he wrote. His teacher sidled up to me and whispered, "Michael isn't one of the writers, normally." I asked her what she meant, and she pointed to three or four others who had covered their papers with words and letters. To those children, writing had become relatively easy. Some of the others were still struggling with the shapes of the letters and the sounds that go with them; and still others were not yet ready to take on writing, but were content to draw.

After a while I went to check on him again. I noticed that he had written first, and only after his words were on the page was he ready to draw. This is a major step. It indicates his sense that he is now able to get across meaning using words alone, that the drawing is nothing more than fun fluff, decoration, a nice plus, and no longer necessary.

What Michael had written was this: "i lk va prt ab fo montns."

The blends, understandably enough, stump beginning writers, who explain, "I don't know the letter for that sound yet," or simply ask, "How do you spell *the*?" Some children, however, make the sound *th* over and over, moving their mouths experimentally until the perplexing sound becomes something more familiar, *v* or *f*, depending upon whether the position is voiced or unvoiced.

I picked up the story and read it out loud: "I like the part about the mountains."

It blew his mind. He glanced quickly at his teacher, who had come up behind me. "You read it," he said, and she did. He socked himself in the forehead. "Oh, man!" he moaned, "I'm a writer!" He grabbed his paper and spent the rest of the class period moving from friend to friend, showing them his work.

"Read it to me," we heard them say again and again, bless their hearts. And read it he did. Two of the children read it to him, and he glowed.

As teachers, we can only help each child discover the potential to make meaningful symbols. This potential is a human birthright. We are born with a brain capable of making symbols that stand for actual experience; we are born with brains capable of abstracting these symbols and organizing them syntactically. Language, mathematics, physics are all born out of this underlying characteristic of the human mind. We do not really teach our children to speak, to write, to think. What we do is even better; we literally stand behind them giving them courage to discover their own power over themselves and their worlds, the power that comes from within.

Having Something to Say

Children are willing to learn to write when they feel they have something to say, and children learn best when they are willing.

It is not our responsibility as teacher, parent, or adult to supply children with "something to say."

It is our responsibility to support them fully and lovingly in their own quest. Applause, helium balloons, flowers, celebration!

Stand in awe of your children, and be grateful for what they have to tell you. Listen when they speak, listen when they write.

They are doing something very tender, very important.

They are bridging the gap from heart to heart.

Mysterious Symbols

I cannot think of a more important book on how children learn to write than Lucy McCormick Calkins' *Lessons From A Child*. If you aren't familiar with it, you should be. It's an elegant, clear, and lovely work. After you read this one, you might want to check out *The Art of Teaching Writing* by the same author.

To the preliterate child, writing is pure magic. The child knows writing means making letters. She knows there are at least several different letters. She might even know that letters get clumped together and that these clumps are where the true magic is. Mom and Dad read a bedtime story; how do they know exactly what words to say, and in what order? Because the writing tells them. It reminds them of the story, even if they have never read it before. The child believes that the word inscribed on the page contains and calls out the spirit of what it means. I believe this too. I write the word *table*, and before your eyes, one appears.

This kind of magic has, to a child, a sanctified quality. A child will play at writing in the same way he will play at house; in an attempt to unlock, enter, and understand the mystery.

A child plays at writing by imitating what he sees an adult doing. Crayons or markers replace pens or pencils; a large tablet, the tablecloth, or the wall does as well as the yellow lined legal pad Mommy scrawls on when she is writing. The child scribbles, scratches, and creates a line that moves this way and that way, like a snake's trail. He murmurs to himself what he is writing: "I'm going to look inside the box . . . what do you see? I see a kitten." Or comments to himself on the act of writing: "Now it goes up high . . . lalala . . . and now I write a letter lying down." The child believes he is writing, believes he is capturing the spirit of the words with his crayon.

Moreover, he believes it because he is not drawing. This is an important point. Drawing is a symbol-making activity, as is writing; but in the act of drawing, the child is making clear to himself and to his readers what the nature of the text is. Drawing is purely mimetic.

Writing is an abstraction, harder to conceive, harder to execute. When the child exhibits a desire to write, she is showing her teacher and her family that she has begun to think abstractly.

Learning to write takes the following direction:

1. The child plays at writing, scribbling invented letters busily while murmuring.

2. The child grasps the idea that there is a closed set of letters.

3. The child grasps the idea that each letter is in some way connected to a sound.

4. The child learns the shapes of some letters through imitation. Certain letters are often confused (p-b-d; m-n; f-v; l-r) and letters are very often reversed. Letter shapes are generally learned hand in hand with their sound. Vowels are always the last to be learned. *O* tends to be the all-purpose vowel. Long vowels are often correctly used.

5. The writer scribes the initial sound of the words in the text. "I W T Z Y" can mean "I went to the zoo yesterday." The child will often be able to "read" the text to the teacher at a later point in time; the initial letters act as a prompt to memory.

6. The writer hears and scribes the final sound in addition to the beginning sound of most of the words of the text. The middles are often left out.

7. The writer begins to fill in the missing auditory information.

Writing is a slow and painstaking process; a single word contains a lot of action. It is extremely difficult for a young child to remember all at the same time the shape of the letter, which letter means which sound, and where he is in his sounding-out process. Letters very often appear out of order, sometimes wildly so. Yet, by the time a child has reached the final step, the initial and final sounds are usually correctly placed, like polite bodyguards at either end of the raucous word, keeping an orderly control over the chaos within. Beginning writers will overcompensate when they arrive at this point in their understanding. It is not unusual to find writers who attempt to sound out every single particle of sound in a given word, because they do not yet know that as a culture we have mutually agreed that certain sounds don't make a difference in meaning. Thus one child writes "ujzuhule" for *usually*, correctly hearing a *j* sound preceding the *z*, as well as an aspiration (*h*) in the middle of the word. Give it time; it comes eventually.

In recent years I have encountered more and more kindergarten teachers who teach their children to write letters in cursive first. While this presents, to the adult eye, a rather disturbing visual effect in the early stages of writing—cursive *r, s, b* hanging unconnected in the air—it has a very practical use when the young writer reaches the point of sounding out middles. With cursive, he can hook the letters together into a whole. This serves three purposes:

1. The child will be much less likely to reverse letters. This will aid him later when he wants to read what he wrote or progress on to read something another child composed.

2. It provides a visual manifestation of what the child knows and feels on a gut level to be true: each word is a self-contained whole. Just as a table is a whole, complete thing and doesn't include the bowl of cereal that has been spilled on top of it, or the floor onto which the milk is dripping, the word *tabl* written in cursive in the child's hand shows the complete name for the complete thing.

3. Relatively complete words composed of a string of letter sounds hooked together by cursive will encourage the child to allow space between words, thus aiding in his own, as well as the teacher's, reading of the work. A child who learns the alphabet as discrete printed letters will be much more likely to squoosh the text into one long stretched-out bubblegummy strand that allows no entrance at any point, than a child who learns the alphabet as cursive letters that can't wait to be hooked up with their friends so they can mean something.

Beginning writers start to fill up the paper absolutely anywhere, without regard to temporal order. If they run out of space in the middle of a word, they stick the next letter in any white space they can find, even if it's halfway across the page. (This technique is not unlike the way I balance my checkbook, or the way John Cage composes music.) We grown-ups have gotten used to seeing a sheet of paper that is to be used for writing, as a grid, a temporal map, rather than as a piece of white paper floating in space that could as easily be folded into an airplane or covered with a map or a secret diagonally written code. We have to agree culturally to an arrangement or we will never be able fully to ascertain meaning. This patterning is the last thing the child learns; and when she has grasped it, the next step is learning to read.

What's A Teacher to Do?

One by one, your children arrive at the point at which they are ready, willing, and able to leap into the abstract and symbolic world of writing. This can be a confusing time for you as a teacher: some of your children are ready, others you suspect are ready but stubbornly dig in their heels, stick out their lower lips, and refuse; still others, you are quite sure, aren't to the point where writing is something they can grasp. What's a teacher to do?

Praise them. Your children arrive for the first day of school excited, confused, scared, lost, boisterous, enthusiastic, and lonely. Most of them arrive believing they can write. Whatever you do, don't tell them otherwise! Allow them some time each day to "write," at first in scribbles, then as they learn the cursive letters and their associated sounds as a group, by sounding out. Many kindergarten teachers encourage their children to keep a daily journal. The daily journal does lots of things:

- It assures each child he has something important to write about on a daily basis. Each life is important and worth examining.
- It allows each child unpressured, enjoyable time to enter the world of writing via play.
- It stimulates all kinds of topics for later group discussions or for individual conversations.
- It instills in them the excellent habit of daily writing.
- It permits each writer, at his or her own pace, to leave behind scribbling that lacks sound-letter association but that serves as rehearsal for real writing; and it allows experimentation with sound-letter relationships.
- It assures each child that she is indeed a writer, and a successful writer.

Nothing is more encouraging than recognition and praise. We all need it. You *know* if someone tells you what a great teacher you are, it puffs you up and makes you lightheaded, happy, and (this is important) suddenly full of sixteen times more energy and enthusiasm than you had three minutes before, when you thought no one appreciated you. Face it; it matters what people think. If they think well of you, suddenly you're floating, your toes barely skimming the ground. You become a superbeing, able to take on anything, because you know you can do it.

But if you hear through the grapevine that someone was disappointed in you, or spreading rotten (and I'm sure untrue) gossip, or gave credit you deserved to someone else, you crumple. You go a little heavy and sad and dead inside. It's a bit more difficult to breathe. You assure yourself you're being silly, it's nothing, really. But admit it: it sure doesn't make you feel like taking on a single extra task, does it?

The same goes for your kids, a hundredfold. When they hand you a piece of paper that says "H" on it beneath a drawing of a house, read it back, "house." If you can't read what is written, congratulate them anyway. Loudly, dramatically. You might ask the child if she would like to read it to you. She might say no, she doesn't want to. Let it go; she's saving face, or she's more interested in doing some more writing. Earlier this year a spunky kid shoved a piece of paper into my hands covered with letters. There was no illuminating drawing to give me a hint. I tried my best, of course. "Oooooo-h," I cooed, "Just look at this! All these words! Great job." Pause. Throat clearing. "Ummm. Would you read it to me?"

The kid fixed with an ironic look. "No," he said briskly, "because I'm only five and I can't read yet." Pause. "But I sure can write!"

There is a good chance, however, that your young writer will read his work for you, if he can remember what he wrote. When he gets stuck you can help by gently, reflectively sounding out the initial letter. Don't push. Too much focus on the forgetting will assure him that he can't read, and since it's his writing, that he also can't write. Remember: confidence at this point is the name of the game. With it, a beginning writer will go forth fully armed. Lacking it, he will fall and fail, and eventually become unwilling to get up to try again.

Spelling

It is absolutely important that you not be concerned with "correct" spelling at this point in your students' development. Spelling, after all, is only a convention. The dictionary tells us how most people spell a word and how most people pronounce it. It does not tell us the "correct" way to spell a word, because in truth there is no such thing. There is only the most popular way, or the way powers-that-be prefer.

Given time, and the proper encouragement, your kids will gradually learn the conventions of spelling. For the time being, if a kid hears a hard *c* sound (as in *cake*) and wants to spell it with a *k*, let her. She's right; that's the sound the letter makes. If she neglects to put the *r* in *bird*, don't worry about it. Next time maybe she will hear it. Under no circumstances should you force vowel clusters (as in *coal, learn*); silent *e* at the end of the word; *th/ ch/ sh* clusters; or any other form of "correct" spelling. Right now, the point isn't learning the rules of conventionalized spelling all at once, but rather being able to hear and identify some of the sounds in some words.

As an example of how detrimental an over-emphasis on spelling can be for young writers, I remember how a well-meaning substitute teacher made twenty-three kids, as well as me, feel discouraged. We had had a pretty good discussion about secret hiding places in the story circle. Everybody had a different idea: some kids wanted to hide high in a tree, others preferred the dark basement, or a closet where the bottoms of the dresses sway against the top of your head. One little girl delighted me by explaining she hides in the tall singing grass when the sun is hot and a tickle of sweat goes down her cheek. After a lot of group discussion, we discovered that the source of her "singing grass" was the hum and buzz of insects! Everyone was anxious to get to the writing table. One by one I questioned the kids and dismissed them to go write. One by one they began to scribble and murmur under their breath.

The substitute was young, enthusiastic, and, unfortunately, misguided. She whipped around the room like a blue-jeaned cyclone, taking away crayons in favor of pencils ("You should be writing, not drawing") and making well-meant but discouraging comments: "I see you've drawn a house. You wrote the letter *H*, but what comes next? No, not a *U*, no, no not a *C*! *OU*! Don't you know that?"

One child had proudly and quickly written: "I hid en u tre en lefz." (I hide in a tree in leaves). I had watched him do it—and noticed that he was keeping a sharp eye on the sub's whereabouts. He busted to get his words on paper before she arrived, so that she couldn't stop him. I admired his spirit and his intention. Unfortunately, what both he and I feared would happen, did. She swooped in his direction, captured his paper—and laughed. "I can't read this," she told him firmly. "Read it to me." Both his heart and mine cracked a little. He clamped his mouth tightly together and shook his head. She didn't understand that she had been dismissed. Instead, she said "Well, if you can't read it, it's because you need to work on your spelling! You have such good ideas here, but everything is spelled wrong." She took his pencil and neatly printed beneath his cursive, "I hide in a tree in leaves."

I made my way through the jungle of arms and papers and hugs to the sub's side and explained to her that we don't worry about "correct" spelling here. I told her everyone had something important to say and that they were encouraged to listen to the sounds *they* hear and write them down. She nodded brightly, and my young writer—who had been listening—seemed a little happier. But a minute or two later, I caught her on the other side of the room, gently encouraging another child to "Listen carefully . . . tre-e. Do you hear it?" She was so concerned with what she believed to be the importance of correct spelling, that she was going to "help" each child "hear" the sounds that go with each of the written letters if it killed her! I wonder how she would handle a word like *psychologist*?

Of course, each child represents a special case, and as much as is possible, each child should be considered in light of his needs and abilities. Each kindergarten class has two or three children who are far above average writers and readers. These kids do need a further challenge on your part. They may be ready to learn some of the rules that govern so-called "correct" spelling. They may be ready for *th/ch/sh* blends. They will ask you questions or indicate their own dissatisfaction with their spelling. By giving these students the help they need to go a little further with their work, you will be insuring a continuing interest on their part.

Take Matthew, for example. He's an exceptionally bright boy, and exceptionally nice. He has knobby knees, always wears plaid shorts, never has a smear of chocolate, catsup, or anything unidentifiable on his face, wears Clark Kent style glasses, and reads like a whiz. When it was his turn to have his eyesight checked, the doctor told him to have a seat and look at the chart.

"Read me the first line," the doctor said.

Matthew did. "Fat," he said smoothly, arched his brows, and awaited further directions.

"No, no," said the doctor. "Read me the letters you see on the chart."

Matthew looked at the chart, looked at the doctor, looked at the chart. "I did," he said finally, after he had double-checked. The doctor looked at the chart, the same one he had been using for years. The top line said *P-H-A-T!*

In another class there is a kid who is known as "Jenny-the-reader." She bears the name with pride, and is always willing to read a book to the rest of the class if there is a spare moment. Jenny's class collectively made a story about a genii and some magic wishes, in which the genii got tricked but deserved it. It was a swell story, and the kids wanted to get together to share their individual work after the circle ended. Some children had drawn, others had written. Several of them had combined drawing with writing, scribing the first sound of each word only. One boy got up and showed his picture, but could no longer remember what all those letters stood for. He scratched his head and handed me the paper. I scratched my head, too. Someone suggested Jenny-the-reader, who modestly took the paper. She looked at it briefly, then read in a piercingly clear voice: "Bapgorfronkl." She paused for a moment to let the story sink in, and then she added, in nearly perfect imitation of me, "You wrote 'Bapgorfronkl,' Jeremy! That's great; you did something no one else did!"

Parent Volunteers, Who Make All Things Possible and Sometimes Botch Things Up

Parent volunteers are wonderful, as I'm sure you'll agree. They make things possible within the classroom that would not be so otherwise, and they make your life infinitely easier. They are generally enthusiastic about helping the kids learn to write. That's great; a parent in the classroom can become a delighted audience to a young reader, a one-person cheering section for a child that needs just a little extra encouragement, a prompter of questions. But please, spend some time with parent volunteers first. Make sure they understand the process children undergo when learning to write. Keep an eye on any visitor to the classroom—parent volunteer, friendly neighbor, uncle, politician, whoever. Do not allow anyone, no matter how well-meaning, to correct a child's spelling. Do not allow any of your children to ask "How do you spell——?"

Instead, your kids can ask for help in sounding out the word. The adult "helps" by repeating back to the child the word, sound by sound. But it is up to the child to identify the letter that goes with that sound. If the child misidentifies in such a blatant way that it is clear he isn't paying attention or is getting lazy, the helper can repeat the sound for the child to try again. The key is patience. Please be sure your parent volunteers understand what is helpful on their part, and what is destructive.

Being Playful

Playing is learning without the pressure. Children play at being adults, play at fighting, play at reading and writing, play at building houses out of pebbles and sticks. When they enter the world of total fantasy, in which the objects that surround them become mentally transformed into something useful for the play, they are also working. They are in effect practicing. They are trying out different approaches to the job at hand, and reviewing the results. A child who is "writing," even if what you or I see is a scribble, is teaching herself how to hold and control the marker for a use other than drawing; she is teaching herself as well that writing is meaningful. If you listen, you will hear her talking to herself about what she is writing. She is magically compressing her vision into a dark squiggle on the page. She is teaching herself to be powerful.

Kindergarten children need a writing-conducive environment. Your classroom should have writing tools available at all times so that children who are playing or have completed other work can help themselves without special permission. Encourage your children to be playful in their writing. Come up with games that incorporate writing, and encourage them to come up with games. On the following pages some suggestions are presented:

Non-competitive Spelling Bee

A spelling bee can be a voluntary activity. Divide the players into two groups of exactly equal size. If you need another player, you or another adult can volunteer. Have a box of stars or hearts or stickers ready. Make two lines of children. Assign a word to the first child in one line, and let her sound it out however she can. She gets a star on her forehead; not for trying to spell the word (correctly) but for sounding it out as she hears it. Then the first child in the second line spells a word. Pick fun, silly, exciting words: *elephant, gorilla, toothpick, scoobiedoo, vanilla*. Challenge the adventuresome, self-assured children, and be gentle with the ones who are less sure of themselves by offering words like *bat, dog, sit, pipe, late*. Be prepared for the entire group, both teams, shouting out letters to the child who is spelling the word. This is fine, everyone is playing. But you, as teacher, should only listen to the letters the speller chooses. The point is, everyone succeeds, no one fails. Everyone gets a star, and at the end of the game, when you count the stars both teams won, you will discover, much to everyone's satisfaction, that it was a tie!

You might have a particularly aggressive speller who shouts out the answer lickity-split before anyone else has a chance. This is a problem, as no one else can spell (and learn) with him around, and soon no one will bother with the effort because they know Timmy will have an answer before they have the first letter. You and Timmy will have to have a talk. Maybe you could give him a special job, like thinking of new words each day for the spelling bee. Ask him to write out a contract or agreement, which you will both sign, in which he agrees not to spell for other people, and you agree to let him select and read a book to the group once a week.

Letter of the Week

Each week, teach a new letter and review the letters you have already taught. Have ready a box of peel-off labels. Encourage each child to label objects in the room that begin with the letter (or sound) of the week. More than one child can label an object. During M week, for example, expect the map to be covered with labels that read *mp, m, np, map, mop*. Writers will get very funny with this one, crawling underneath your desk during U week to leave a label, labeling their own foreheads with "Me!" during M week. Once you have completed the letters of the alphabet, which will be well into the school year, go in for the blends, just for the fun of it: *CHalk, CHair, CHange; SHoe, SHoulder, SHaker; THings, THroat.*

Another letter of the week project is to compose a story all about the lettersounds:

> Once there was a boy named Jimmy who went to the land of J. The first thing he saw was the planet Jupiter, it was big and huge. Jimmy jumped on Jupiter and then he met a jellybean. Jimmy and the jellybean saw a big jet just zooming overhead, and so they jumped into the jet. The jet flew so fast that they fell out; they fell down and down, yelling "Gee whiz!", until suddenly they landed in a Jaguar. Before they had a chance to go anyplace, a great big giant appeared and stepped on the Jaguar containing Jimmy and the jellybean. The Jaguar got jammed, and the jellybean got squished absolutely flat; it just lay there and jiggled. Well, Jimmy jumped up and hid in the giant's pocket. The giant was on his way to visit his friend who was a jokester. This jokester liked to tell jokes and sometimes juggle. The giant laughed and laughed, and when he laughed, Jimmy got jiggled around in the giant's pocket. The giant laughed hard, and Jimmy got joggled out of the giant's pocket and jumped into the jokester's pocket. The giant told the jokester to juggle, and so the jokester reached into his pocket and juggled two balls and a tomato. Then the giant said, "More! Juggle more!" And the jokester jerked Jimmy out of his pocket and juggled him too. He juggled him so hard that Jimmy went spinning through the air very fast all the way to June. When he got to June, he landed *kersplat* in a jar of Jell-o and he got stuck. He had to stay stuck in the Jell-o junk until the giant got hungry and decided to eat him. The giant jammed Jimmy into his mouth, but Jimmy's shoes were dirty, and the giant opened his mouth and sneezed! Jimmy got sneezed out and went spinning through the air to . . . (you finish the story!)
>
> —*Mr. Brennan's kindergarten, Bell Top School*

Kid Sandwiches

Once several letters have been learned, make small sandwich boards out of cardboard. Cut a piece of thin cardboard into one-foot-square pieces. Using a paper punch, put a hole in the upper left and right corners of each piece of cardboard. Don't put the holes too close to the edge or they will eventually rip out. Now, use bright thick yarn, and tie the two pieces of cardboard together with enough slack so that a child can wear the sandwich board over her shoulders. One piece of cardboard should fall in the middle of her chest, the other, in the middle of her back.

Scribe out a letter in large, dark cursive on the front of the sandwich board. On the back, scribe out another letter. You will need to make at least five sandwich boards bearing two letters apiece for this project to work. As your class learns more letters, make more boards. Eventually, you will need to repeat letters. Put the sandwich boards in an accessible play area.

Here is the game: four or more children can play. One child is the speller, and does not take a sandwich board. The other children each don a sandwich board so that one letter is in the front and one letter is in the back. The speller, usually with a lot of vocal help from the letter-wearers, arranges the children in different orders to spell out words. If three children are wearing boards, he will have the choice of six letters (a child can be turned around to make her backside letter usable). Thus, with the letters *b, t, o, i, m,* and *k,* the speller can make several words:

bot (boat)   bit (bite)   tim (time)   kit (kite)
bik (bike)   Tom   tok (took)   bok (book)

This game is an exercise in reading as well as in writing, because the speller (and his helpers) have to sound out the letters as they go along in the construction of the words.

Hidden Letters

As the class's knowledge of letters and their associate sounds grows, incorporate another game into their daily activities. Hide pieces of paper around the room on which have been scribed a single letter of the alphabet. This is a good one to get parent volunteers to help with, as writing out and hiding all those pieces of paper can be time-consuming. Children will collect letters as they find them hidden inside their coat pockets, stuck in their lunchboxes, underneath the globe, and so forth.

When a child has collected enough letters to sound out a word, he or she can glue or tape them to a large piece of paper; e.g. the letters *b, d, r* once collected, can be arranged *b-r-d*, or "bird." Each day, review the words each child has collected thus far. Encourage each child to try to discover a story/sentence that could be made out of the collected words. Thus, the child who has taped

     brd   sit   flr   fli

can cut out the individual words (now backed to paper with tape) and arrange them to read; "brd fli flr sit" (The bird flies to the flower and sits.)

The above exercises are good confidence builders, and they are fun, besides. They show the kids that they have the ability to be masters of letters, to arrange them into meanings that they control.

What is even more important to the beginning writer, however, is the realization that they have something to express from their own experiences and feelings. The journals, previously discussed, are good for this. Here are some other ideas:

Mailboxes

Place three mailboxes in the room. One is for school mail and can be used to house incoming and outgoing letters to children in other classrooms, principal, librarian, kitchen workers, and other members of the school community. These messages should be placed in envelopes and addressed to the receiver.

The second mailbox is for in-class mail. This one is for the messages to and from one class member to another, or to and from parent volunteers or visitors.

The third mailbox is world mail. This one holds letters or messages to television personalities, friends who live across town, relatives, and other members of the world community. These letters will have to be stamped. The child can address the letter on one side of the envelope, and the teacher and child can together address the letter on the other side of the envelope, where the stamp will go. Writing and mailing letters will also increase your class's motivation to communicate.

Drawing/Writing

As previously discussed, the story circle can be used to generate a text from each child. Following the group story, each child returns to his work table to draw a single scene from out of the story. He can then label objects in the scene, script a statement about his drawing beneath or alongside (or in some cases, across!) it, or choose to skip the drawing altogether in favor of a written text. This approach is especially useful for several reasons:

- It allows each writer to proceed at his own pace, without pressure and without frustration. For some children a drawing plus a single letter is sufficient. For others, three or four sentences are sufficient.

- It gives every child a feeling of confidence and success whether the drawing stands alone, is accompanied by words, or the words stand alone. In itself, drawing is also a symbol-making event.

- It allows a practice for writing. As the child draws, she is considering what she will write about. She is focusing in on her subject and clarifying her thinking concerning it. She draws a picture of a pond. "This is the part about the water," she says to herself. She adds a cat. "And then the cat goes in, *kerplop*. And yells." Now that she knows her subject, she is ready to begin writing about it.

- It acts as a stimulation for writing. Once she has completed the drawing and begun to write, if she forgets where she is, all she has to do is look at the picture and she will remember. She writes, "watr ez weht" (the water is wet); another child appears and asks her a question. They laugh together for a moment. She returns to her work. "Oh, no," she wails, "I forgot what I was doing!" Then she looks at her drawing and her text. "Okay," she says, "I didn't forget." She writes, "cat falz en ghts wt" (The cat falls in and gets wet.)

Drawings accompanied by written text don't have to be generated only by group stories. Children should be encouraged to draw/write in their journals, in messages that go into the mailboxes, on the chalkboard. Here's another project I have found five-year-old writers like:

What's Inside?

Each child draws a picture of a building—house, castle, fort, office building, whatever. Or, it can be a picture of an outdoor place—the woods, the ocean.

The child puts several large doors and windows in the drawing.

The teacher and helpers cut out three sides of the doors/windows so that they can be folded back to open and close. Each student then tapes a second piece of construction paper behind the first piece. When doors and windows are opened, the student draws and/or writes behind it the object or name of the object that is hidden there. For example, a haunted house might show a skeleton dancing behind the front door, a bat or spiderweb in one window, a ghost in another.

Drawings of nondwellings can also show doors in the most unlikely places: a tree can have a door that when opened reveals a squirrel. A flower can have a door that hides a bee. The ocean can have a door behind which fish swim. The sun can hide the moon behind its door.

Books

Eventually, as your kids become more and more comfortable with writing, they will want to try their hand at books. Books are great for lots of reasons. After they have been shown how to construct a book (instructions follow), avid writers can make and compose two or three a week. Books encourage a narrative, chronological sequence. Something happens on page one, followed by something else on page two, which leads to something else on page three, and so forth. This sequencing provides the opportunity for dramatic development, something that a single sentence written beneath a drawing doesn't do. The book, when finished, is a source of great pleasure and satisfaction to the young writer. He knows writers write books; he has written a book; therefore, he is a writer. Books can be made fancy by replacing the front and back covers with cardboard, wallboard, or another stiff paper product, covered with Contac paper or wallpaper. Books bear the author's name proudly and right up front. Books encourage research and reflection into any subject.

On the last day of my residency in one school, each child in all four kindergartens constructed and wrote a book on a subject of his or her own choosing. Some kids wrote about nature: caterpillars and butterflies, trees, gardens. Some wrote about an event: when I lost my tooth, when I got lost at the circus, when I went shopping. Some wrote pieces of fanciful fiction: the haunted turnip, the penguin's house. One little girl decided her subject would be dead bodies! At first I thought she was trying to get my goat, but when I questioned her to see what she knew about the subject, I discovered it was a sincere interest on her part. For several days she had examined a small rodent that had been killed by her cat, studying it like a scientist for signs of decay until what remained were nothing but tiny bones. Her story began, "vrbud gt bonz" (everybody's got

bones)! She'll probably grow up to be a wildly successful blues singer.
Here is one way to make a book:

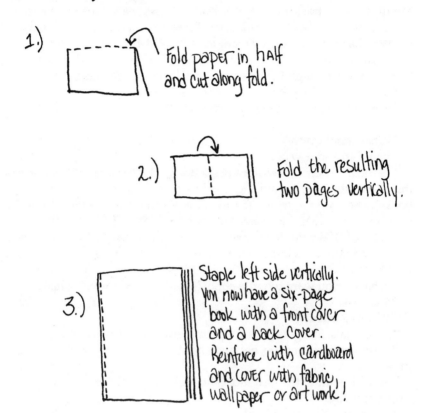

1.) Fold paper in half and cut along fold.

2.) Fold the resulting two pages vertically.

3.) Staple left side vertically. You now have a six-page book with a front cover and a back cover. Reinforce with cardboard and cover with fabric, wallpaper or art work!

You might have your own ideas, or want to expand on mine. Whatever you do, don't assign topics! You can introduce books during the time you set aside for class writing; some kids will be so into their subject that they will choose to pursue it over a few days on their own. You are at the advantage over me here: you know your kids. When I do a six-day residency, I just begin to get the feel of what some of the writers are interested in. We make the story circle, but instead of generating a group story, I tell them that I know each one is an expert on at least one thing. We talk, shmooze, visit, gossip for a while. This is a nice time, this group conversation. Something one child says will cause a spontaneous erup-tion from five or six others, "Farm machinery? Hey, I know all about that! My uncle has a tractor and I rode on it." Everyone is indeed an expert, and experts write books. One by one, I interview them. It goes like this:

"Who has something they want to write about?"

Lots of hands shoot up. I point to one child at a time, rapid-fire because there is never enough time and because their energy and mine is high. We're excited; we're going to write books.

"What's your book going to be about?"

"Caves!"

"What about caves?"

"Bats flap and it's cold!"

"Go do it." I hand the writer a blank book, which I have been construct-ing as we talk (time permitting, encourage your kids to make their own books). The writer scurries off, full of ideas and intent. It's clear from the short interview that this writer knows his subject. If he had simply said, "It's dark," I would have pried further, because that's information everyone knows. It's important to make your writers conscious of what they know.

"What do you want to write about?" I ask the next waving hand.

"Gardens."

"Whose garden?"

"Gramma's. She gots peas and lettuces and she wears gloves."

I dismiss this writer, too, because she obviously has something solid in mind.

"You," I point to the next kid, who looks uncertain, but has her hand raised anyway.

"Gardens," she says. She shrugs.

"Oh, yeah?" I ask her. We pause. "What about them?"

Long pause.

"She got peas and lettuce", she says in a small voice. We look at each other. She shakes her head briefly at me and closes her eyes to let me know she knows I know she hasn't found her subject yet.

And so on. You must be alert to which of your readers is really turned on and ready to go, and which are imitating something someone else said, but also be alert to the fact that maybe four or even five kids do know about caterpillars and can write their own ideas about them.

By the time you've interviewed all the volunteers, there's a good chance you will have two to five kids left over laying on their bellies and looking . . . hopeless. This is your cue to make some suggestions— *not* assignments. Here are some that often stimulate a response:

> lost teeth;   getting lost;   hiding underneath some-
> thing;   watching ants;   singing;   giants;   colors;
> dance recitals

You will find that some children wax poetic; one little boy decided to write a story about a ballerina who danced at night in the moonlight in a parking lot! Others are careful, scientific observers. If somebody in the group experiences writer's block, don't push. Remember; life is fun, and it doesn't need to be anything but for a five-year-old.

Suggest that they do a book that has lots of different drawings. Sometimes, you will discover the formerly blocked child diligently scribing out word after word beneath his drawings! Keep your expectations someplace in the realm of the realistic. There will be times a child reports lots of details and is ready to write, but the book itself might lack the story line the child had begun with, might even lack consistency, trailing off in three different directions in pursuit of three different subjects.

The little boy who intended to write the book about the ballerina who danced in the dark of a parking lot had his details clear in his mind, and that is what is important. When it came to collecting them all into a single book, many of the details remained in his mind and never made the transition to the written page. That's fine; don't criticize and don't push. His book showed a ballerina, with the word *dnkr* underneath her. The next page was completely scribbled in with a black marker. You couldn't read it anymore, but I knew he had first scribed the word *drk*! The next page showed a butterfly. Probably this was an example of peer-group pressure: three other kids at his table were writing books on the caterpillar-butterfly connection. However, when I leaned over to ask him what was a butterfly doing in a book about ballerinas (it wasn't pushing, it was an honest question), he thought for a second.

"I don't know," he said slowly. Then a smile spread on his face and he looked at me slyly. "I think because the dancer goes like a butterfly." With that, he hooked his thumbs together into a classic butterfly, leaped from his chair, and began gently to glide and turn around the room, a dancer indeed, lead by the butterfly of his hands.

One other nice thing about making books. You can save a corner of the room for the library and keep the book collection in it. During the story period, a young writer might want to read his or her story out loud or share the drawings. An avid writer/reader can check out books by other children to read to herself or others at her table. What an ego boost for the author! In fact, once or twice during the year, you could stage a "meet the authors" party, and invite parents, neighbors, friends, and relatives to come for a cup of punch and a cookie and to examine the books or to listen to the authors read. Bring a Polaroid, and snap a picture of each reader to be included in the author's notes at the end of the book.

Childmade Tales

The following stories were created in story circles that I led in the East Greenbush School District. I contributed to the making of the story as little as possible, usually little more than the opening prompt, which was as often as not, changed by the writers. In those stories that retain my original prompt, I indicated the spot in the text where my question ends and their story begins with an ellipses (. . .).

> Once there was a very clever little girl. She lost a tooth and . . . she put the tooth beneath her pillow because she knew the tooth fairy would give her some money. So the tooth fairy came and left money. But there was a problem. This tooth fairy was very forgetful. She forgot the girl's tooth under the pillow. Well, the girl said, "I can make some money from this forgetful fairy," and so each night for the next eighteen days, the girl left the same tooth under her pillow. Each night for the next eighteen days, the tooth fairy came and left money and forgot to get the tooth. Pretty soon, the girl was rich and the fairy was very very poor. The girl bought a fancy car and some new clothes. The fairy remembered then that the girl owed her eighteen teeth, and so she went to the girl's house that night and looked under the pillow for the eighteen teeth, but they weren't there. Then she looked in the girl's mouth, and found all the girl's eighteen teeth there! So she touched the girl's mouth and all the teeth one by one came into the fairy's hand by magic, because the tooth fairy is indeed magic. When the girl woke up she tried to eat her granola for breakfast, but she discovered she had no teeth! So she made herself some pretty paper teeth, and they looked so good when she smiled! But when she tried to eat her favorite food, a caramel apple covered with peanuts, her paper teeth came out of her mouth and ripped and tore. She then got some vampire teeth that were very long in the front and glowed in the dark. They were supposed to be for Halloween, but she needed them now. She could eat her caramel apples but all her friends were afraid of what she looked like and they all ran away. Then she made

herself some teeth out of an old metal can, and they cut through the apples really well, but they were so ugly that old ladies said to her, "you see little girl? You ate so much junk and now your teeth are all rotten looking!" So the girl went home and cried. She decided there was only one thing to do. She put all the money under her pillow and that night the tooth fairy came and took it all. And when the girl woke up, she discovered her teeth had come back, by magic, one by one, into her mouth where they belonged.

—Ms. McIntyre's kindergarten, Green Meadow School

Lost or missing teeth are an archetypal image for young children. Introduce a lost tooth into the action, and everyone gets interested. Lost teeth seem to have some kind of magic associated with them. Don't ask me—a talisman, a type of voodoo? We all know about the tooth fairy from our own childhoods, and in this story, she is the source of the magic. I was tickled by the story's raison d'être; the forgetful fairy who is taken advantage of by a crooked money-grabbing kid. This is a story, finally, about justice. Goodness and justice have power (magic) on their side. If you disrupt the balance of things in a dishonest attempt to improve your life, you will pay for it in just proportion. Your life will not be improved, but made worse. The only way to return to your original position (which is in balance and morally apropos) is by correcting the injustice. Unless you want to end up with paper teeth, heh heh heh.

The wind is a . . . woman with hair as white as clouds. Her pants are made from the red sunset, and her blouse is white and soft like clouds. One day, she wanted jewelry. She already had stars that she wore in her hair, and she took little bits from the sun for her throat and for earrings, but she wanted more. She went to the kingdom in the clouds. When they saw her coming, they thought she was a snowstorm because they only saw her white hair and her white blouse, and they thought she was clouds and snow. When the king saw her he hid, because he knew she wanted his gold. But she sneaked in by blowing through the window. He got cold by her blowing. His lips turned blue and his face grew icicles. He went and hid behind a cloud. Then when he checked his gold, he saw that it was gone, because she had taken it all to make jewelry. All the people on the earth looked up at the sky and saw the wind floating back toward her home carrying the gold. It glinted like gold coins, and they couldn't see her because she was invisible. She lived in the sun, and she put all the gold in her room. But then the sun got very very hot and the gold all melted and dripped through the sun and through the air and fell into the ocean. It looked like sunlight sparkling on the water, and all the people looked at it and said, "It looks like gold."

—Ms. O'Conner's kindergarten, Red Mill School

This morning I got in my car to come here to teach you guys, but...before I knew it, it drove me to a big big house. I went to knock on the door and I heard a big voice yelling "help!" So I pushed open the door and went upstairs where the voice was yelling, and there was a giant laying in his bed. He was yelling for help because he fell out of bed and his head cracked off and rolled underneath the bed. I looked under the bed and there was his head in the shadows, but it blinked at me and rolled out the door and down the stairs, *dumpum-pumpumpum*. Then I went downstairs and the head rolled under the couch. Then I tried to grab it and it rolled out the door, *dumpumpum*. It rolled down the hill and I chased it. It rolled to Chris's house and I saw it in the basement. When I knocked on the door, Chris said "I'll get it," and threw it out the basement window. I caught the giant's head like it was a beachball or somebody's fat belly, and walked up the hill with it. It was so heavy I sweated and got tired. At the top of the hill I put it down and rolled it and kicked it because it was so heavy. I kicked it hard and it rolled fast all the way to the door and knocked over the door and rolled up the stairs and rolled to Googly Ferris's bed. He reached down and picked it up and stuck it back on his head. Only now the head was tiny! I wasn't going to tell him why his head was so tiny, but then Chris showed up and when Googly Ferris said "why is my head so tiny?" Chris said, "When Cynde kicked it all the air came out and it got tiny." So Chris and I decided to jump on Googly Ferris's belly to push air up into his head, and when we jumped on his belly his head got big, then when we stopped jumping his head got little. Then we put pins in his body so that we would let the air out and his body would get little to match his head, but it didn't work. Instead he looked like a porcupine. Then we blew up a balloon and put it in his mouth, but it exploded. We were ready to give up, but then Danny showed up with a bicycle pump. So Danny put the bicycle pump in Googly Ferris's mouth and pumped and pumped, and his head pumped up big. But we put too much air in him and he exploded.

—Ms. Rosano's kindergarten, Bell Top School

Giants, like the tooth fairy, are very popular with the young set. In *The Uses of Enchantment*, Bruno Bettelheim suggests that to the child, giants are nothing more than adults grown into the psychic dimensions the child already feels them to be. You will find that in the stories your children create, whether the giants are friendly or hostile, bumbling and clumsy, or cutting and severe, the child-protagonist will win out. As Bettelheim finds in traditional fairy tales and as I have found in the classroom, the success of the young protagonist is due not to luck or the intervention of an adult, but to the child's own will and cleverness.

Mr. Ferris, incidentally, is the beloved principal at Bell Top school. The kids were tickled by the idea of turning him into a giant, giving him a silly name, and putting him in the story. This story is in fact about problem-solving. While I am one of the characters in the story, I function within it as neither older nor more capable than the other, child characters. And remember, it's *my* fault that the giant's head shrunk! The fact that they explode the giant in the end isn't so much an admission of failure as it is a pretty funny way of securing closure within the framework of the story. It had simply gone on long enough, the kids were getting twitchy, and one of them decided that if the giant was blown up they could get on with other things themselves!

> In the field in winter through the melting snow you can see frost through the tracks. You can hear a deer sniffing the snow for apples. In the springtime you can see green grass and brown dirt and violets growing by rocks. Red tulips are just starting to open and up above the sun is tossing warmth in the blue sky.
>
> —*Ms. Hofmeister's kindergarten, Green Meadow School*

The above piece of writing is thoroughly poetic; in the first stanza (I ultimately decided against writing it out as a poem because the line breaks would have been my own, involving too much interference on my part), the kids have strongly focused on the idea of winter as a covering. Snow covers a field, a track covers the frost. Winter hides things beneath itself. A deer (which is itself hidden, so that we don't see it but hear it instead,) sniffs the snow, which is hiding apples. I love the implied vivid red of the apples against the white snow, reminiscent of W. C. Williams poem "The Red Wheelbarrow."

This subconscious reference to color seems, in the second stanza, to bring it bursting into bloom, heralding spring. Green grass, brown dirt, violets who bear within their name a color, red tulips, a sun we know to be yellow, and the blue sky. Nothing is hidden in the second stanza. Instead there is a sense of opening, accepting, reaching out.

The prompt questions I asked the class were largely concerned with the senses. What did you smell? What did you hear? Look closer, what else can you see? Again and again, I asked them to close their eyes and see a picture that answered my question; a rudimentary version of the meditation exercise. Image is the picture the mind makes, and the more details of sense (sounds, smells, colors, tastes, textures) there are, the more solid, vivid, and effective the image. I asked also for placements: "You can hear a deer," says Randy.

"Doing what?" I fire back. Someone paws the ground. Someone else snorts, and everyone giggles.

"Sniffing," Autumn says.

I nod, look skeptical. "Ho, hum," I say.

"The snow," Autumn adds and watches my face. I keep it blank, waiting, asking without asking for her to go deeper. "For apples," she concludes, and we are both satisfied.

"That's pretty," Jimbo says. He sounds startled.

Everyone laughs, and we go on to make the second stanza. Someone offers springtime as an idea; several people talk about color. We all lean back on our hands and grin, looking out the window at the bright spring day. We are as relaxed as the red tulips, starting to open up to accept the warmth the sun is tossing.

> Once there was a little ghost boy who . . . went to ghost school. He was very sad because all the other ghost children made fun of him. The reason was because he didn't live in a haunted house like they did. He lived in a house under water, in the ocean. Instead of spiders, his house had lobsters. Instead of bats, his house had fish. He didn't like it because every day when he left his watery home and went to school, he squished. His shoes squished, and when he sat down in his chair he squished and left a wet spot on the chair and all the other little ghosts laughed. Well, he decided he would run away from home and find a real haunted house to live in. He did just that. But he was afraid, because when he got to the haunted house, he heard bats squeaking, and he was afraid of bats. He was afraid they would get all tangled up in his body, just like they can get all tangled up in a person's hair. He went inside the haunted house and saw monsters, and goblins, and then he saw Count Dracula. Count Dracula came and grabbed the ghost around the throat. This scared the little ghost so much that he turned invisible. He started to fly, because he didn't want Count Dracula to take a bite out of his neck and suck out his fog. Count Dracula didn't let go of the ghost boy, even though he had turned invisible and was flying through the air. Together they flew straight to the ocean where the little ghost boy lived, and when they plunged into the cold salty water, Dracula let go of the ghost boy's neck because the water scared him so much. He ran all the way back to the haunted house, and the ghost boy ran all the way back to his watery house. He was very glad to see the lobsters and fish and his

mother and his father. "I might be different from the other ghost children," he decided, "but at least I live where I don't have to be afraid!"

—*Ms. Meisel's kindergarten, Bell Top School*

Kindergarten children love a good ghost story. This is one kind of tale where you don't have to keep prying for details. They know the generics perfectly, from goblins to black cats, from skeletons to spider webs. What you do need to do is to make them reinvest energy into the generics, which are absolutely clichéd to the adult mind, but still somewhat fresh to the child's. But you've got to ask questions! The kids won't wander into this kind of territory without your encouragement (notice, please, I did not say 'without your guidance'). Why was the ghost sad? He lived where? How was it different? Remember that for such young kids, context, expression, and gesture are all part of the total communication they will give you in response. When you ask the group, "Why didn't he like living under water? Why did the other ghosts think that was bad?" No child, no matter how articulate, is going to answer, "He didn't like it because everyday when he left his watery home and went to school, he squished." Instead, someone will fill his mouth with spit and make a squishing sound. You ask them to be more specific: "He squished? Where?" The answer could be "his feet" or "when he flew" or "school." Listen to the answers, verbal, gestural, or dramatic.

Today is Meagan's birthday. This is a story about the birthday party Meagan is going to have after school.

Meagan invited all her friends to her party. She invited the loudest boy in the school, but she didn't know he was the loudest. In fact, he was the loudest boy in the world, but she didn't know. He got there first. When she answered the door, he yelled HAPPY BIRTHDAY!!!!! and the windows all fell out and broke and all the things fell off the shelves. Meagan put the books back and cleaned up the broken windows. She Superglued together the broken glass bird that fell from the shelf and she did a good job but the fingers from her left hand got stuck to her other arm. So the loudest boy said, "you did me a favor by cleaning up when I made a lot of noise and broke things, so I will return the favor." So he YELLED!!!!! And the Superglue got scared and came unglued, and he yelled so loud that Meagan's teeth jump out of her head and ran sideways into the dark closet and hid under a pile of dresses. Then all the other kids showed up for the party, and Meagan couldn't talk to them because her teeth were gone. Then her teeth missed her and crawled out from the closet. They were wearing a dress so nobody would know they were teeth. The loudest boy in the world saw a dress walking across the floor, and when the teeth jumped out and jumped into Meagan's mouth, the loudest boy was startled and SCREAMED!!!! so loud that everybody's teeth jumped out of their mouths and into the air. The teeth floated through the air and fluttered like butterflies and got into the wrong mouths. Some people with little smiles had big teeth and some people with big smiles had little teeth.

—Ms. Kelly's kindergarten, Green Meadow School

Each child in your class deserves a group-made story on her birthday. After the story is told, kids can draw and write birthday cards. The birthday story can be set in any location, and usually involves a lot of slap-dash high-jinx humor. Notice the motif of teeth; familiar from a previous story.

Additional Storytelling Ideas

Here are some themes and ideas that have worked well for me in the past. They can either become the core for a group story, or your kids might prefer to write something on their own. By no means should you limit yourself to this list or feel as if you are forbidden to change these suggestions or keep just part of them. As a creative writing teacher, you need to be constantly alert for what turns your kids on, what doesn't move them in the slightest, what areas of interest could be delved into for material.

Hiding Places

Everybody has one, adults too. Is it indoors or out? Where exactly? Picture it clearly. What do you hear? What can you see from your hiding place?

Portraits

Especially good for individual writing. Relatives are good here, but strangers are even better. Probe for details, and discourage the ever-ready and ever-boring *nice, fun, good, pretty, scary, mean, ugly, silly*. Where is this person? What are they doing? Tell me one tiny little thing you see, and one great big thing you see on or near this person. Each child's piece should be different, even if writing about the same person. You can do this assignment as a natural follow-up to a field trip, or even a walk around the school. Go look at the kitchen ladies, really study them. Look at the mailman's knees when he comes to bring the office mail.

Found Objects

Something from home, something found outside, something from your purse! Look at colors, smells, tastes, other qualities. Again, avoid *nice, good, fun, pretty,* et cetera.

Folktale

Group story about the things that occupy the sky, the woods, the ocean, the seashore, an island, or any other place in nature. These stories involve basic personality types in conflict. Objects are given human characteristics, and allowed to work out their problems. Can be a good problem-solving story.

Fairy Tale

Giants, magical helpers, objects that talk or act human, things disappearing, flight, magic of all kinds. This type of story is almost always sure-fire. Give them a character, ask a couple of questions about the character's feelings and why, and let them take it away.

Houses and Other Dwellings

Tree houses, tepees, holes in the wall, mouse houses, nests, a flower's house. Dwellings can serve as the story-starter/setting, or they can contain the basic problem for the story's eventual resolution: a mouse that lives in a nest, for example, or a flower who lives in completely the wrong kind of house for a flower. Let your kids determine what kind of house is wrong for the mouse or the flower. It will be enough if you simply suggest "He lived in the wrong kind of house. He lived in . . . ". This age group loves dwellings and can be very imaginative about them. You can drape your room with sheets for a giant tent effect for this story if you want.

Places

A lengthy group discussion about places. Discourage place names: they are handles only and don't conjure any image or details. Where in New York? What building? Describe it, what did you see there? Press for indoor places—room, closet, underneath spot, attic, car interior—and outdoor places—meadow, field, pond, rocky ledge, athletic field, baseball diamond. Press for details of weather; weather completely changes a place. You can write as a group or as individuals about the same place in two (or more) kinds of weather. Ask for details involving the senses. You can write about the place without any people, if you want. This usually results in quiet, meditative pieces. Nice for a rainy or sleepy day.

Morning Sounds

Or evening, or any other time/location you choose. Brainstorm with them: sounds made by animals, sounds made by machines, sounds made by human beings, sounds made by your own body, sounds made by nature. Again, these are often very lovely, thoughtful, creative pieces.

Who Lives Inside a Stone?

Read, for your own pleasure, "The Stone" by Charles Simic. In fact, read, for your own pleasure, everything you can find by Charles Simic. You can introduce a study of rocks, crystals, and minerals for this writing assignment, too.

Twins

Magical or otherwise. One good, one bad? Or maybe the two work in tandem in some kind of wonderful way. Does the teacher know they are twins?

One Day, a Pencil, a Banana and an Old Shoe Went for a Walk . . .

Or any other weird combination you can think of. A list of odd objects doing something either mundane or bizarre.

Dolls Coming to Life

As much as I cringe at the plethora of sentimentally conceived brand-name dolls on the market and in most homes today, the truth is, to the kids they are real and alive. Since they are alive, they can have adventures or problems just like other people.

The more group stories you make, the more journal writing, drawing, writing, and books your children do, the more quickly they will decide they can find their own topics to write and tell stories about. A little creativity generates a lot more, and it spills like sunlight through the rest of their lives. Creative people are in motion, are productive, enthusiastic about their lives and minds, and happy. They love easily and healthily, and they are fun to be around. They seem to handle their own lives better. It's important to give children the tools for their own joyful existence.

A Review

You're convinced that kindergarten is not too early to start a creative writing program. You see that a child who has been encouraged to think creatively will enthusiastically embrace the means by which her ideas can be made immortal—through writing. You have seen in your own classrooms the process learning to spell takes. You believe, with me, that traditional methods of teaching writing discourage rather than encourage thinking, learning, creativity, and writing itself. These include copying from the board, filling in workbook pages, and all those methods we grew up with. So, you're ready, willing, and, I have no doubt, very able to proceed.

Creative writing in the kindergarten classroom can and should take two distinct but interrelated forms. The story circle is a community effort to which everyone can contribute. It is very low-stress and insures automatic success and confidence. Because so many minds are at work, brainstorming away, it generates some surprising and terrific ideas, which in turn stimulate further ideas from the contributors. Story circles can be used to generate stories based on reality, or fanciful, fun stories. Individual writing is sparked by the stories the group composes. Everyone is turned on, and the fact that everyone is writing about the same thing—the story—means that there is a sense of community support. At the same time, each writer chooses a different point in the tale to write about; thus, individual creativity is encouraged. You can read the communally made tales included in this chapter to stimulate your kids. They are sure bets, as they were kidmade with very little adult interference.

As well, there are numerous ways to encourage individual writing. Some I have discussed:

- **Daily journals**
- **Letters or messages to people within the class, people**

within the school, and people in the world outside the
school
- Labeling objects in the classroom that begin with the
letter of the week
- Games: spelling bee, hidden letters, and sandwich
boards boldly scripted with one letter on the front, one
letter on the back
- Art projects, such as the one that incorporates doors
and windows that open to reveal hidden messages

3

First and Second Grade: Building Courage

Comforts of the Nest

Children enter the first grade armed with a sense of what writing is and does. In kindergarten they have become acquainted, and many have begun a love affair with the written letters of the alphabet and their accompanying sounds. With the right amount of encouragement from their kindergarten teacher, they will burst through the first-grade door brimming with excitement for what they know they can learn—to write with power and with grace.

Just now I was interrupted by a terrible commotion outside—squawking and the furious flap of wings. By the time I reached the window in my tree-high house, the first of the nestlings I have watched for weeks had leaned so far forward on the branch that it was forced to leap into thin air. It dropped nearly to the ground, then gained control of its awkward wings. With a lot of flopping, it made its way back to the safety of the nest. But then the wind lifted its feathers, and it was leaping and gliding once again, this time a little higher. Each time it had the courage to take off, because it had the nest waiting for its return. Each time it returned, it missed the feeling of independence, freedom, flight; it missed the feeling of potential and nature fulfilled.

My own wild imagination took over as I watched, turning the little bird into a frantic but greatly enthusiastic kid—tooth missing in the front, arms flapping and little bare feet kicking. Then I looked up into the lush green depths of the tree, and I saw you, Teacher, the mother bird, flapping your wings and yelling loud praise and encouragement.

There are two things you have to do: provide the nest, and help them toward the courage to leave it as, one by one, they are ready.

Story Circles, Take Two

The story circles I described in the previous chapter on kindergarten can be applied to your beginning-of-the-year first-grade group as well. The story circle is a place of comfort and acceptance for all. The shyest has as important a position as the most bold. The creative child can provide the forward motion to the narrative, and the practical child can fine-tune the details. The poets among your kids can lend the whole a style and an atmosphere that suffuse the story with just the right feeling.

Story circles are fun. But they also serve a very definite purpose. They give your kids a belief in themselves as storymakers. Each child is indisputably a member of the community and a co-artist in the making of the story; at the same time, the story, to an important degree, reflects and contains her. The story circle is thus doubly secure—a sturdy nest in a high, safe tree.

There is a third contributing factor to the sense of security the story circle gives. No first-grade child feels sufficiently articulate to spin a story from beginning to end. For one child's magical story beginning to work, other children are needed to provide the middle, the end, and all the rich and delicious detailing. But because the fictions produced by the story circle are absolutely kidmade, the classroom feels the presence of a meta-author, a Big Kid that lacks a body and speaks through twenty-three mouths. The Big Kid offers something for each of your real kids to strive toward—becoming that wonderfully articulate artist who can create a powerful story from beginning to end.

First graders may bear certain similarities to their kindergarten selves of the previous year, but they are not the same people they used to be; therefore, the story circle has to be tailored to their needs. If you are lucky enough to inherit kids who are already familiar and comfortable with the story circle from the previous year, use it to your best advantage. Even if you have to introduce the technique to them, you will discover that their blossoming independence will quickly bring them to the next stage.

In the meantime, you've got a lot of territory to cover. Introduce your kids to their own rich and varied imaginations, and help them to realize how they can shape and form lasting stories. Explore all different types of fiction: stories of magic and magical people, folk tales, tall tales, ghost stories, stories whose themes come from "real" life, comedies, stories from other cultures, stories involving talking animals or misplaced animals. The list is as endless as you choose. The more you do as a group, the wider the visions the children will later bring into the second stage of first-grade story circles—the circlets.

Circlets

After a month or more of daily group stories, it's time to encourage your kids to work by themselves in smaller groups of three to five. At first, they will need a grown-up to get them started. Primarily, they want you there to bail them out if they get stuck. If you use student teachers or parent volunteers, *be sure they understand the theories behind the story circle.* Train them yourself, ask them to sit in on a few full-class group stories first. This is very important. A well-meaning but overly enthusiastic grown-up helper can quickly deplete the group's creative energy and even convince the less-confident kids they can't do it themselves. Little by little, the grown-up, be it you or a helper, should begin to drop out verbally, offering fewer question prompts, fewer verbal clarifications, fewer gentle reminders. Eventually, the grown-up will only need to make a single prompt-question: What is your story going to be about?

Because you are simultaneously helping your kids learn to function as socially healthy individuals, you need to establish certain rules of acceptable behavior within the smaller story circles. Ultimately, the circlets will provide the young writers with the chance to create kidmade stories out of their experiences, fantasies, ideas, fears, and hopes. This will only work if the circlet knows how to function fairly and smoothly. Everyone in the classroom must collectively consider and decide upon certain behavioral parameters. Again, encourage your students to make up the rules. Post the guidelines someplace in the room, maybe in a corner reserved for the circles. Add rules as needed. Some things to consider:

- ❧ People leaving or entering the group are a distraction. In addition, the joiners don't know where you are in the story. Ask for a rule concerning drinks and "I gotta go to the bathroom."
- ❧ Everybody has good ideas. How can the group keep from getting into arguments about whose idea to use?
- ❧ How do you decide who should be group leader?

    ❧   **In a small group, should you raise hands, go around the circle**
        one by one in turn, or speak out as the spirit moves you?

I suggest that you allow the circlets to have an ever-changing character. You don't need to group the same five kids together into the circlet once and for all time. However, you might want to establish the same groups for the first two weeks or so, while you, and they, are working out the kinks of cooperative writing without adult supervision.

One more thing to keep in mind: the stories that are entirely generated from a small group of kids will in all likelihood not have the sophistication of one that is crafted by the entire class and the adult who acts as the Big Editor. Don't expect them to. A story that might seem a little bland to you, or a little lacking in logic in its narrative sequence, or in some other way not as richly detailed as a group story, is just as deserving of pride and praise.

Use What You Know

How can it be possible to make daily time for the story circle, or for creative writing, given everything else you are expected to cover in your school day?

Use the story circle for everything it's worth. The making of the stories themselves can reinforce other study areas. If you are undertaking a study of plants, do a story about a plant that thinks it's human. Encourage the kids to bring real information into the story. Where do baby plants come from? Why do we cultivate plants? Are all plants edible? Whatever you are studying—be it any aspect of the natural world, human society, math, or reading—the story circle can be a tool. Even a story that is about fantasy and magic needs to incorporate real details from our human experiences. This is an important aspect of creating fiction, and the earlier the child writer grasps it, the better. A fantasy story in which none of the details are grounded in the mundane, daily world of our experience leaves the reader/listener with nothing in which to anchor her imagination. A fantasy story about, for example, chickens, in which eggs play a central part, will delight and amuse the reader/listener, because she knows about eggs and can compare real-world knowledge to the eggs in the story. Eggs can crack or scramble in real life; in the story, such a fact might have everything to do with the unfolding of the plot. Conversely, perhaps the egg in the story has a shell harder than cement, and that might be central to the story action.

I begin big-group stories about hidden or secret doors with a brainstorming session on what we, as a group, know about doors. The kids always surprise me with what they know. Here's a list one group came up with:

> Doors keep the inside in and the outside out.   You can lock them to keep your money and your stuff safe. Some doors aren't for people, like garage doors, pet doors, mouse holes, and cupboard doors.   Doors keep the wind out of the house.   They keep the warmth in the house.   They keep noise out of the room.   They let you have a place to get away.   If you don't have a lock, put up a sign that says *Do Not Disturb* and nobody can get in.

A story can be created by the group which has, as its raison d'être, the violation of one of the above facts. In violating one or two of the rules, however, the others must be reinforced as irrefutable facts. To violate all of them would create a muddy story that gives the reader/listener no truth of experience in which to believe. One class did a perfectly charming story about a house in the middle of the woods that did not succeed in keeping the inside in and outside out. The owners at one point come home to find grass growing where the carpet used to be and gently rolling hills replacing the stairs.

Writing Is Dwelling

I have already talked at length about how stories generated by the story circle stimulate in kids the urge to draw and write. Drawing/writing is an activity that makes the story permanent; it gives the amorphous tale a physical text, a body that can be examined, reexamined, and referred to later on. It's quite literally a charm against forgetting. A child will refer to a drawing and some words hung on the wall and say, "Oh yeah, I remember that one about the duck that couldn't waddle," and all the details will come flooding back.

Writing and drawing are activities that allow you to dwell in a certain state of mind and heart. Dwell—what a gorgeous word. It means to abide, remain, linger.

Dwelling is delicious. When you, as an adult, close the cover on the last page of a moving novel, you don't immediately jump up, slap your hands together, and announce to the cat and several browning avocado plants, "Well, I guess I'll do six months' worth of laundry now and make Boeuf Wellington for dinner!" Hell, no. You sigh, flip idly back through the pages, letting your eye linger on a phrase here, a word there, remembering. You wish the book weren't over; you feel a little bittersweet. And you feel momentarily at loose ends. You need something to help you transit into the other, exterior world. So, maybe you scratch the cat, who is now in your lap and pawing at your hand, and then you get up and wander around the room, straightening things here and there. Gradually, the mood eases back, and you are ready to move on to the next thing.

Ditto with your kids. They are literally *inspired* (comes from two words that mean "to breath in") by the stories they have made with their own breath and whose atmosphere they have been breathing. They need an activity that will allow them to dwell within their imaginations a little longer while helping them make the transition to the exterior world. In addition:

- Drawing/writing allows each child to work at his own pace. Some kids will leap right into composing a pictureless, complex text. Others will need to use the drawing as a practice and for a reminder later on.

- Drawing/writing establishes the link between mental creativity orally expressed, and writing. A regular drawing/writing time following each orally produced story will help the classroom be comfortable later on down the line, when you encourage them to create individual stories directly onto paper without the intermediate step of a group-made, oral story.

- Drawing/writing allows each child to dwell in what was important to him as an individual. Drawing/writing allows each child to make the group activity relevant to the individual.

- The kids are excited by their own creativity and inspired to write. It's a great opportunity for you to help them feel that they have something from out of themselves to write about. People who feel they have something important to say are a lot more likely to put out the energy to write it down than those who don't.

Growing Confidence, Growing Independence

In first grade at the beginning of the school year, just as in kindergarten at the end of the school year, the excitement of telling an oral story as a group leads to the confidence to write as an individual. Many of the same techniques and story ideas suggested in the first chapter for teacher-writers can be brought by the first-grade teacher into her classroom.

Daily journals, portraits of family members or of strangers (the beautician, the ice cream man, the lifeguard), a memory (getting lost, getting stuck, finding something), and so forth can all become material for stories. Some children will want to take as their subject a story that has already been told by the group, and rewrite it in their journals. Others will insist upon finding their own subject in their own way.

You will no doubt have some writers in your classroom who are wildly turned on by one particular genre or theme. Ghost stories, stories about a popular or favorite doll or toy, Transformers, space stories, and so forth; you know the kids I'm talking about. I think you will find that, at least early on in the school year, children who opt to write realistic works based on experiences in their own lives will be less likely to become distracted, stuck, or disinterested. Stories based solely on the imagination tend to bog down a beginning writer. I am absolutely not suggesting that you try to steer writers who are working on individual pieces away from more fantastic subject matter. I am suggesting that you keep a sharp eye out for scrunched up faces, wandering eyes, bubbles blown from spittle, and the kid who gets up six times in a row for a drink. These guys need help. An alert teacher can bail out distracted, ungrounded kids by doing a quick, image-provoking meditation with them, or by asking direct questions.

Meditation

In the first chapter I told you about how many years ago I accidently discovered, in a class that was wildly out of control, how useful meditation could be. As a prewriting tool:

- It allows a transition from group activity to concentrated individual work.
- It directs each writer inward, toward the source of her own creativity and imagination.
- It provides images as subject material, thus acting as a prewriting dry run.
- It helps remove performance pressure by focusing attention on the process of creation rather than the product created.

Besides, it's fun. Young kids are especially eager and willing to shut their eyes and close out the distractions and worries of the world for a while, in favor of enjoying a personally created, richly detailed movie. You can use meditation prior to story circles or prior to individual writing. Your job is to act as the Questioning Voice. Your responsibilities are similar to those of a kindergarten teacher who asks her children prompt questions for the weaving of a group story. Your job is not to tell them what to visualize, but to suggest non-specific material and ask each writer to provide the details, the language, the heart and the creativity to simultaneously make the story his own and bring it to life.

Turn out the lights, put up a *Do Not Disturb* sign, and lower the blinds. Pick your subject ahead of time, but remember, you are making only the vaguest of suggestions. You are giving them a scaffolding on which to build. First, ask them to breathe quietly and deeply two or three times. Be sure to allow a moment or two between each breath, or they might get dizzy. You may need to emphasize the quiet part. Then simply ask them a few questions of a fuzzy, vaguely suggestive nature:

- Picture yourself in a place. Where are you? What do you see on the ground or on the floor? What is it doing? You hear some kind of sound. What do you hear? Look and listen carefully. You are the only one who knows these things. It's up to you to notice everything.

- You are standing in front of a small object. What is it? Look at it carefully. What do you see? Pick it up. Something happens. Things are changing. Everything is becoming something else. Look carefully. What is each thing becoming? Where are you now? What happens next?

- A long time ago, when you were very young, something happened once. You remember. You remember. What was the air like, what was the weather like? Who was with you then? What happened? Remember everything. It's inside of you to remember. See it all.

- There's a person you see every day, but you don't know this person's name. Can you picture him or her? Where do you see this person inside your mind? Put your hands back down, and don't answer me with your mouth. Just make a picture inside your mind. Look at this person carefully. Exactly where are they? Remember three things about the place where you see them. What sounds do you hear? What can you smell? What is this person doing?

With meditation, pacing is everything. The point is to help the kids get relaxed enough to lose themselves in the images they see. They have all the time in the world. When your students have their heads down and their eyes closed, they are completely open to you. You must let them linger for a moment with each image your question conjures.

Ask a question.

Pause.

Breathe deeply yourself. This is a time for you too.

Take a step or two. Ask another question.

Expect yourself to be uncomfortable the first three or four times you do this exercise with your class. It's a whole new way of relating to them. You might have a little stage fright, or you might feel stupid. Its okay to feel those things, but tuck them back into a little unused corner of your mind and proceed. If you try this with your whole heart four times and you still don't like it, you don't have to do it anymore.

You can use meditation with an individual or a very small group as well. If the class is writing but two or three of your kids are having trouble, or if a couple of kids want to write, let's say, a ghost story but don't have any real ideas, get them to meditate. Quietly ask the writers to put their heads down and breathe deeply. Ask them to visualize a picture of what it is they are going to write about. You can help them over the hump by telling them not to make up a picture, but to *find* a picture inside their minds. Assure them that they know what they are doing, that you know they know. Ask for details, particularly of sound and smell and touch. The individual meditations are real quickies; you don't have to take more than a minute or two. If your writer pops up in the middle of a question, don't scold. It means you helped and he's ready to write.

What's Meant but Not yet Said

In addition to or instead of meditation, you can help an ungrounded writer by asking specific, direct questions about the writing she is doing. The effect of this is similar to meditation in that the questions you ask act as reminders. However, with direct questioning you are looking for verbal answers. You ask a question, your little writer answers. Equipped with the information she gives, you ask another, more specific question. The questions can be used to clear up foggy, ambling areas in the story action. They can be of a sensory nature, asking for details of sight, smell, touch, taste, or sound, or they can be questions that delve into character motivation: Why was the rabbit angry at the cat? Once again, your questions are designed as prompts to the writer's imagination. Be very careful not to take over, due to a misguided desire to relieve the child's frustration, and be very careful not to lead the child toward an idea you think would be great.

I had a conversation with a teacher a while ago that I thought about for a long time because it was so distressing. She was a very high-energy, very enthusiastic person. I wasn't working with her class, much to her disappointment. We talked during our mutual breaks in the teacher's lounge every day. She told me how much her kids like to write, and what great stories they did. She radiated excitement and enthusiasm, and when she told me that she'd had the kids put their stories on computer disk and had made a booklet, I asked to see it. She sure was right: the stories were stunning. I've worked with kids for many years, and I know what they are capable of. I also have a sense for what they aren't capable of, developmentally and experientially. Every so often a kid sails through who is nothing short of a Shakespeare in Transformer T-shirt and dungarees; but when I saw the stories in this booklet—*whew*—I was ready to throw in the pencil.

"Did they do these on their own?" I couldn't keep the jealous whimper out of my voice.

"Absolutely." She nodded and looked proud.

"Did you have to prompt them?" I tried not to cry.

"Oh, sure," came the reply. "It's a special class and their handwriting isn't all that good and sometimes they hand you something you can't even read, or you can read it but it doesn't make any sense at all. So you have to ask them, what did you mean here?"

"Uh," I said, beginning to catch on, "and then you write down what they said, like taking dictation, word for word?"

This brought peals of laughter. "Oh, no!" She snorted gleefully. "They'd go on forever! You have to stop them when you get an idea of what they're trying to say. You have to say to them, 'Do you mean this? Is this what you're trying to say? How about we word it like this?' and then you get them to agree and then you write it down and then they're finished with their story and you can get on to the next kid."

Whew. I guess they would be finished with their story, and probably finished with the desire to make stories from here on out.

A word of caution: don't expect too much of your first graders. For some, a single sentence is all they are able to do for now. For others, a page is not outside reason. They might demonstrate orally that their creativity is high and their visions strong; but for first graders, when it comes to getting it on paper, a lot might get lost. This doesn't mean that you are asking too much in the first place, nor does it mean that they have either lost interest or are lazy. What it means is that they are in process, they are learning about their own abilities to invent and about their own capacities to be in technical control. Praise their efforts, whatever they may be.

The Writing Folder

From the beginning of the school year, I suggest that you keep a writing folder for each child. Under absolutely no circumstances should you allow the only copy of a piece of writing to go home. Xerox or hand-written copies can be made for writers to carry home to the folks. Stress this to subs and helpers. You and I know stuff that goes home, no matter how responsible the child or her family, can get lost, eaten, used by the cat for litter, or folded into a paper airplane by a cruel older sibling. If you keep all work in a folder, it will give you, the parents, and the child a chance to see how work has progressed over the year. With a year's worth of writing, you can see areas in language skills in which the child needs help, you can see special areas of interest that might otherwise get overlooked, and you are better equipped to make recommendations to the second-grade teacher.

The writing folder can be a businesslike manila office folder, legal size; a folded-over piece of heavy construction paper; a cardboard box of uniform size, like a shirt box, one per child; or anything else you can come up with. Of course, your kids will want to decorate or write on the folders, to make them their own.

Making Happy Messes

When your kids are writing a story, they are working very hard. They are simultaneously holding an image/idea in their minds, remembering letters and associate sounds, reviewing what has happened in the story, and rehearsing where the story is going to go next. The last thing you want to do is to make them nervous about spelling and penmanship. Encourage them to sound out words as they go along. Encourage them to cross out mistakes and just skip over the mess. The word on first drafts, for you and for them, is Don't worry about it. It's their ideas that count for now.

Even More Ideas to Work With

Ideas for individual writing are everywhere. Your kids will come to school daily, armed with a zillion observations or daydreams that could become the seeds for stories. For your first graders you can use any of the ideas I suggested in the section on kindergartners. Some of the ideas I offered for your own writing could be tailored to suit your kids, as well. Daily journals and memory books stand out as the two best possibilities for this age group. But do not attempt stream of conscious, automatic writing, or dreambooks with them. These areas are beyond their understanding at this point. Here are some more writing ideas.

Sequencing

Set up a lot of dominoes around the classroom. Tap one so that it falls into the next, which then falls into the next and so on. Talk about cause and effect with the group. Discuss how when something happens, it can make something else happen. Give some examples:

When I fall down, I skin my knee.
When I eat too much, my stomach hurts.
First I kiss mom good night, then I go to sleep.

Play a game of "first . . . then . . . last," listing five things out of order which must be put in order by the kids. Ask for volunteers to give a cause and effect. Incidentally, the terms *cause* and *effect* are obviously too sophisticated for this age group. Talk around it: "Can anyone think of something that makes something else happen?" Fire makes your hand burn. A flat tire makes the car wobble. Too much coffee makes Mommy hysterical. A hug makes me happy.

Cartoons

Your kids will be able, without much urging, to make a comprehensive list of all kinds of impossibilities. People can't fly, dogs can't sit at a table and read the paper while drinking coffee, things can't disappear magically into thin air and reappear in the Grand Union. Spend some time coming up with a long list of absurd sillinesses—walking on water, flying, defying gravity, objects that act alive, people that don't. Insist that your kids give extremely specific suggestions. Don't write anything down until you are satisfied with it. Then, once the list is complete, tell them they are free to use anything they can come up with, even if it isn't on the list. In fact, it's even better if it's an original.

Next, hand out a very large piece of paper to each kid. Show them how to fold it in half length wise, then up and down, thus making four squares:

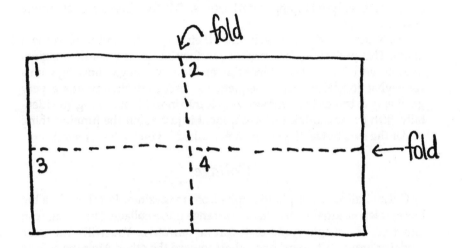

Instruct your kids to number the squares from one to four (either direction).

Square #1: They will draw a picture of anything they want, in any place they want, doing something. This can be very weird. A lamp in a pizza parlor doing the cha-cha? Go for it. Two pigs wearing sneakers swinging in the playground? Why not? Underneath the drawing is room to write a few words or a short sentence about the picture: "The lamp eats pizza and dances."

Square #2: They draw/write the next thing that happens to the character, be it animal, human, or thing. The scenes can transform with dream-like inconsistency, but there is some cause/effect in place here.

Squares #3 and #4 proceed sequentially.

In all, move them through only four prompt questions about what happens next. It is entirely possible that you will have to try this assignment with your kids once or twice before they will catch on.

My very favorite, made by a student many years ago, is yellowed with age and resides on my refrigerator, the place of honor in my house. It shows a dinner plate on which there is a porkchop, some spaghetti, and a stalk of broccoli. Underneath, it says, "I not hengry." Then in the next drawing, a huge hand comes down and takes the plate away. Underneath: "Mom is mad." Next, (this is the great part) the broccoli has turned into a tree, the porkchop has righted itself and is trotting off in prehistoric-dinosaur fashion, and the spaghetti is wriggling wildly around the corner. Beneath it is scripted in jagged dark letters, "My food beecam live!" Yowie zowie.

The kids love to show each other their sequences and to read them aloud. This project tends to produce cartoonlike pieces, wildly imaginative and very funny. It combines the reminder of a single drawing with a somewhat logical narrative sequencing discussed already. It's a very good way to bridge from the story circle into individual writing. (Incidentally, fifth graders think this assignment is just about the funniest thing under the sun, but sixth graders are insulted if you try it on them.)

Collage

Cut out all kinds of photographs from magazines. Put them in a big box and let the kids choose them to arrange into a collage. The collage can either be of a single scene or it can be narrative. You will find some students gravitate toward one, others toward the other. After the collage has been assembled and glued, give each student a separate piece of paper to write a story about what's going on in the collage. Keep away from famous TV, movie, or music personalities. Your kids will become locked in to what they know or have heard through the grapevine about the person or the show the person represents. The later it is in the school year, the more sophisticated these stories will be. Early on, you might get one or two sentences of a fairly mundane nature:

> The snak on a roc.

Remember, your kids are juggling an awful lot; they might not have the skills to say what it is they are thinking, but they are working on it. By the end of the school year, the same child might be able to write:

> The snake sits on a rock in summer. He can take off his skin by wiggling in grass. He sounds like somebody whispering.

The Emerging Artist

Second graders stand at a threshold midway between their younger, more innocent selves and who they will become—worldly, wise, and clever. Second graders like a good joke; they also have a developing awareness of their individual emotional lives and a sympathy and empathy for one another's. They turn to the family for society less and less, toward the community of other kids more and more. While kindergartners and first graders see storymaking as a kind of delightful game, to the second grader, especially later in the school year, a story is a consciously expressive and artistically wrought act. Second graders are that much more adept than first graders at the skills involved with writing. They have learned, in the previous year, to spell many commonly used words, to sound out words whose spelling is unfamiliar, and to retain in the mind's eye the images and words that are about to be captured on paper. Their stories can therefore contain a great deal more sophistication. They are full of facts and love to answer the Big Question—Why?

The Second-Grade-Tailored Story Circle

As with kindergarten and first grade, the story circle should be introduced at the beginning of the school year. Besides being a fun way for the group as a whole to get comfortable with itself and to get to know its disparate parts, working within the context of the story circle establishes confidence in kids who might otherwise experience a quaking heart at the idea of writing.

But second graders are very opinionated and independent. The story circle will rapidly spark a desire to make individual stories. Return to the story circle on days when you think they need it—sleepy, rainy days, the occasional afternoon when nobody is getting along or working very well, or when the class gets giggly and you can tell they would best channel it into a collective effort. For the most part, however, after the first two weeks to a month, the creative writing your class does will most likely be as individuals.

Journals

Daily or weekly journals are a very good idea. These can be kept separate from the writing folders I suggested in the section on first grade. It isn't necessary that you, as teacher, check each entry; in fact, it's more respectful if you don't. Stress this to the kids:

Journals are for writing whatever you feel like writing. No one will

correct the spelling or anything else. You can invite a friend or a
teacher to read your journals if you want, but you can keep them
private if you prefer. You are in control of your journals.

The only rule should be that to prevent loss they should remain in
school and are to be taken home under no circumstances. If a child wants
to share a section at home, Xerox copies can be made. Encourage kids to
write about ordinary experiences in the journals, as well as those that
spark excitement. If a member of your class brings in a salamander,
suggest she write about where she found it and how she caught it. If
someone is learning to make dried-flower Christmas wreaths, suggest he
make notes on the process in his journal. Journals should not be reserved
for pieces of writing that reflect only the good in life, either. A child who
has gone through a traumatic experience—the death of a grandparent or
parent, the loss of a pet, a car accident—will sometimes choose to use the
journal to come to grips with his feelings. The following remarkable
pieces of writing were dictated by a first-grade boy. He asked me to write
down his words, because, he said, "I have important things today and I
can't do all the words." His father had died only two weeks before:

> My mom drew her handprint on a piece
> of paper. She wanted to keep it.
> I flushed it down the toilet last night.
> I don't know why I did it. I didn't
> like it. I wasn't mad. I went outside
> and rode far away. I can't ride farther than
> Lyon's funeral home where my dad got buried.
> I went by it anyway, up to Joshua's. He
> wasn't home. I rode back home. My mom thought
> I was next door. She went grocery shopping.
> I found a turtle in the woods a few days ago.
> A girl knocked on the door and asked for it
> back.

The next day he wrote:

> My dad died October 1. He got
> drunk. That's when he died. He
> was in his bedroom. My aunt found
> him at noon, laying in bed. He died
> before I got home from school. I
> felt sad, like people can cry. It
> had to happen because it happens to
> everybody. There were a bunch of flowers
> at the funeral. I didn't know a lot of the

> people. They were crying. I cried. There
> were a whole lot of flowers on his grave.
> Bees attacked the flowers.
>
> —*Jeremy D.*

Never insist, however that a child who has had a trauma write about it. Some kids deal very well with the events of their lives, no matter how upset we think they should be. Other children simply might not be ready yet to deal consciously with what we, as adults, think they should come to terms with now in the hopes that it won't build up on them later. Besides, you might be wrong, like I was once.

I was working with a group of young kids who were telling a group story about a singing lamp, a tennis shoe, and several other assorted objects that apparently had souls and personalities and who lived together on the moon. One very quiet, morose girl added to the list of nonhuman moon dwellers, "my pappy who died and went up to God in Heaven."

I froze. I was responsible for a whole classroom of little kids. The notion of death, and even more upsetting, the death of a parent, had been introduced by an obviously unhappy child. Should I stop everything and hug the poor girl, urging her to have her feelings, assuring her I was there for her, helping her to get it all out? Or should I proceed as if a dead pappy was the symbolic equivalent of a singing lamp, and integrate him into the story along with all the other personable misplaced objects on the moon? I glanced at the teacher, who looked worried. Well, since the girl wanted her dead pappy on the moon, she must have some reason, arbitrary, deeply complex, or otherwise. So, we integrated the dead pappy into the story. As the tale progressed, other children embraced the dear departed, suggesting narrative details that included him as well as the other objects. The little girl brightened considerably with the telling of this tale, and I felt proud of myself, as if I had somehow helped her with the rest of her life; as if, in spite of myself, I had been wise.

As soon as the story was finished and the flock scampered back to desks to do their individual writing, I took the girl gently by the hand. We went to the back of the room, where I asked her if she wanted to talk about her pappy. She shook her head; her eyes brimmed. I asked her if she wanted to write about her pappy so I could understand what she was thinking. She bit her lip and a tear fell. I cursed my youth and inexperience, I cursed my insensitivity and lack of psychological insight. Worried now that I had scarred her for the rest of her life, I laid a piece of paper in front of her. Would you like to draw? Yes, she would. Tears turned to sunshine, and I excused myself to hastily confer with her teacher, who hovered nearby, as anxious as I was. Teacher assured me this was the first she had heard about the dead pappy. The girl's mother had never mentioned him. In fact, it must have happened a while ago, because the girl's mother appeared to have a husband who was both alive and well.

Soon, we were hailed by the girl. "Come see," she called, "I drew Pappy!" We nearly knocked each other over in our haste to reach her side. There, upon the paper, was a house with a curl of blue smoke, a large green tree, a little girl much like our little girl . . . and a fat white kitty beneath whom she had written "papy."

Ghost Stories

Kindergartners like to shiver with delight, clutch one another's hands, squinch in as close to the teacher as they can get, and tell a good ghost story—as long as it's out loud and all together. First graders like a group fright as well, and think of it as a nonthreatening game. First graders like to tackle ghost stories on their own, as well as in a group. It's a subject they know well, and they are sure it will draw a good audience. Second graders, though, consider a solid ghost story just about the hottest thing since microwave popcorn—and they would rather either tell individual stories around a pretend campfire or write individual stories to read aloud to the class.

Campfires are easy and you don't have to worry about smoke. Get a battery-operated extra-strong flashlight, a lamp, or a lantern, and several pieces of crunchy red and orange transparent paper, the kind that looks like stained glass. If that isn't available, you can use red and orange tissue paper almost as successfully. Crumple the paper up and arrange some of it around the base of the lantern, where light will catch it. Tape the rest over the light itself. Collect enough sticks to give one to each child in the class. Pass out marshmallows (be sure to check for diabetics or nonsugar eaters, don't ask them, ask their parents), two per kid; more than that and they get hyper. You can either tell a collective ghost story, let kids storytell ghost stories that are classics, or encourage individuals to make up a ghost story from start to finish while the group listens and occasionally asks questions.

Sometimes just planting the idea—"Tomorrow we'll do ghost stories"—is enough to get them going. This poem was written during free time before we were slated to tell ghost stories. Ginny was so proud of it that she insisted on reading it first thing, while I set up the campfire for the rest of the group:

The Ghost

One day I went
to a old spooky house
I met a ghost there
we became friends
right away. I brang
him to school
I did not know that
they can turn
invisible and he
would get me
in trouble
but he did
get me in
trouble by
tickling me
and made
me laugh
I told
my teacher
but she
did not
believe me
and she
sent me
to the
Principal.
The
Principal
did not
believe
me
either
so he
sent
me home
and my
parents
did not
believe

me either
I was
mad at
the ghost
he did
not mean
to do
anything
but he
did do
something
to me
he said
he was sorry
I know you did
not mean anything
but you did do
something. I am
sorry little girl. And
they made up
and they are friends forever.

—Ginny I.

Not only is Ginny's subject matter typical and of definite interest to a second-grade class, but she uses writing creatively to express an issue of major concern to the average seven-year-old—justice. Seven-year-olds like rules very much, especially those related to society and community. They believe that what they have been taught about proper and improper behavior is absolute and inviolate truth. Nothing is more alarming to a seven-year-old than to be told "Life isn't always fair." Ginny's poem is about getting in trouble for something someone else did. The fact that the ghost is invisible only adds to her problems. On a deeper level, the poem is about not being trusted by adults, which is something all seven-year-olds feel at some time or another, sadly because it's often true. When she feels betrayed by the adults, even by the Principal, who is the symbolic judge in the eye of the child, she turns to her peer—the ghost who got her in trouble in the first place. There is solace in this turning, for after justice has been restored via the ghost's apology, "they are friends forever."

Ginny arrived at this shape all on her own. Notice that at the beginning of the poem (her word for the piece), when she is still working out her ideas and not entirely absorbed in her work, the lines are fatter, more sentencelike. This shape is apparent at the end of the poem as well, when she is returning to her self. Note, too, that she switches to third person at the end, as if she is no longer active in the relationship or in the story but watching it from a narrative distance. She becomes the storyteller, finishing it neatly and forever.

Real Stuff

Fantasy and imagination trigger images loaded with symbolic value for the young writer. In writing about ghosts, the issues of fear, disruption, injustice, or any other of a number of possible disequilibriums in life can be tackled. In my work, I occasionally run across a teacher who insists that her children only write narratives or poems about reality. In my experience, however, magic, giants, talking animals et al. *are* part of a child's reality. They offer a safe forum for exploring issues and solving problems that are otherwise overwhelming. In *Uses of Enchantment*, Bruno Bettleheim discusses this issue in fascinating and articulate detail.

Then there's the "real stuff," aptly named by one of my second-grade students. He was a down-to-earth kind of guy, squarely built, utterly kind and fair with the other kids, and completely uninterested in occupying a fantasy world. "That's for babies," he explained to me once. "I like the real stuff." Like this poem by Tina:

> The sky is blue
> I hear foot steps I am
> frightened. I run in the house.
> I can still hear foot steps.
> I fell down and it stopped.
> I got back up again it started.
> when I stopped once more and it
> stopped. I ran to the garage
> and I heard it more.
> My heart started to pound faster.
> I seen a light shining in
> My eyes it almost blinded
> me. And I turned around
> the light was not there.
> I ran out. I ran to the road
> to see if I could see the person
> was there. I yelled who is it
> I stood there for a minute I
> seen a shadow in the garage
> I heard a record player
> I went upstairs the

record player it was not
playing I turned around it
was my cousin Lise
I asked her why she did it
she said what I said you
know and we heard a noise
we ran to see who it was
we ran upstairs we hid under
the covers we were shaking
my dad and mom and her mom and dad had a flash
light I said to my dad
it was you all along

—*Tina T.*

The above poem contains more suspense and fear than the previous ghost story, which wasn't designed or told to terrify. Tina is utterly in control of her detail throughout the poem, from start to finish. Her opening line, "The sky is blue," is a factual if mundane observation that presents us with a normal world from which we are about to radically deviate. The closing line, her accusation to her father, "it was you all along," signals a return to the familiar world where logic keeps things in their proper place. Notice, too, that she only tells us once that she is "frightened," and then, only after giving us just cause for her fear. Sound detached from logical cause plays a big part in the fearfulness of this poem: footsteps falling, but no one is there; a record player going, but it isn't turned on. Visual effect divorced from logical cause is also present: shadows in the garage, with no reference to what is casting them; a light that nearly blinds her, with no explanation of what or who is shining it.

Tina was worried about reading this out loud to the class because she understood its power and didn't want to frighten anyone. They begged, though, and she read; and elaborated.

"Did that really happen?" someone asked.

She nodded, but added, "but I made up the part about the robbers in the garage."

The class looked confused. "What robbers?" somebody else protested.

It was Tina's turn to look confused. "Oh," she said, "the ones I didn't put in!"

Sequencing

For many second graders, as for most first graders, the logical sequencing of narrative events is ofttimes skewed in a story. A story based on real-life experience will spill detail willy-nilly, appearing in the retelling in exactly the same order in which it appeared in the writer's mind. First and second graders do not naturally revise; what is written is written. The following exercise works especially well coupled with a meditation on a memory. You can lead a meditation about a particular type of experience shared by everyone (remember once when you got lost?; remember the time you broke something you wish you didn't?), or you can encourage each kid to reach into the well of his stored life and choose his own. The memories do not have to be dramatic—a fire, an accident—but can be a simple, peaceful moment, something remembered for no apparent reason.

Ask the writers to number a paper from one to ten. After the meditation, they will write down a single piece of the memory they recalled, next to each number. Remind them to go in order as much as possible. However, if somebody gets mixed up, she can always go back and renumber the paper.

Nightmares

1. I always thought when I was four I saw a white glove doing weird things
2. It arm wrestled me I won but it was hard
3. I always thought my blankets were moving
4. I saw a big black thing out in the hall
5. I screamed as loud as I could when I saw the black thing
6. I ran out and turned on the lights but didn't find a sign
7. Sometimes I felt like I was falling off a cliff when I did my dream went blank

—*Adam M.*

This poem's seemingly effortless ability to exist in the interface between dreams and reality very much reflects a young child's mind. Adam reached into his dreamlife with his own hand to wrestle with a white glove. In fact, if it weren't for the title and the context provided by the rest of the poem, it would almost seem as if Adam had reached into his dream and pulled the glove out to the external world. Although the poem is pretty scary in its precisely envisioned and carefully crafted details, Adam himself was amused by it. The narrator of the poem is himself, an older boy, who looks back at his younger self as gullible and wildly imaginative. However unconsciously, Adam the artist has carefully sealed the distance between his two selves in the poem's perfectly seamed end. There is no doubt, given the strength of the image of the final line, that he is still more than a little affected by the memory of the fear of death.

Sledding

1. One day my friend and I were sledding
2. We had ice in my red sled
3. We were sledding on a steep hill
4. We saw a barbwire up ahead
5. Kyle my friend yelled barbwire ahead!
6. I yelled try to steer away from it. I can't Kyle said
7. The barbwire was a foot ahead of our heads we ducked under
   and didn't get hurt

—Robin W.

In extending the dramatic space in which the poem unfolds by giving us a lot of satisfying sensory detail (ice in the red sled, the steep hill, the approaching barbed wire), Robin imitates the action of the poem, waiting until the last moment to provide us with the last piece of information. As Robin and Kyle duck under the barbed wire, in our minds, so do we.

Later if he decides to bring the poem into another draft, Robin can choose to remove the numbers. They are useful in the first draft both because they help him to organize his thinking and his time sequence, and because they subtly prepare him for something we will discuss later on—poems and their shapes.

1. I remember the day when I first learned to tie. I was three years old and I was in bed. My quilt had strings on it. I tied two of the strings together.
2. I called my mother and father in to come and see what I did.
3. They came in and turned on the light and said you are learning very fast.
4. But then they turned off the light and went back to bed.
5. I tried to do it again but then I got tired of doing it over and over again.
6. And then I went to sleep.
7. I was dreaming about tieing my shoe.

—Amber J

I love this for its perfect balance: it's a flawless memory about a very important, but usually forgotten, event. Amber is also a careful student of psychology; in the poem, she manages to capture the child's attempt to magically control her parents. She learns to tie, practicing over and over with the materials at hand. When she succeeds, her parents appear to congratulate her. But alas, they then turn out the light and leave. She ties again and again, but doesn't succeed in drawing them back, and so she sleeps—only to dream about her new-found power!

Falling Through Ice

It was very, very cold.
I jumped out in a flash
It was right by the dock
It was in the middle of January
I ran up and changed my clothes very fast
I had my winter jacket, hat and gloves on
I didn't want anyone to know
I kept it a secret till it was night time
I climbed up the side of the dock to help me out
I thought it was thick ice
I used a broom to check it first

—Adam M.

After writing his nightmare poem Adam felt that he understood the shape a poem can take well enough to order his thoughts without numbers.

Night Life

A lot goes on at night, both inside a kid and outside the house. Get your class involved in a discussion of night sounds, shadows, stars, camping, or something else having to do with night. I had fun with a class in North Rose once.

It was in the days of spring when the weather had just begun to warm enough for the early peepers to come out and shimmer like bells. When I arrived at the second-grade classroom, more than a little delirious with spring fever myself, I found the kids deep in an impassioned group-babble about the incredible insect racket of the night before. I listened for a while, and asked a few questions. Someone asked if they could meditate about last night, because it had been so pleasant the first time around:

The Night Peepers

Every night we come home from the baby sitter's we hear the peepers. The peepers chirp through the night. It sounds like they were talking to us. They sound almost like crickets. I like the sound they make .... Every night we go on the porch to go in the house it seems like they're right behind us having a conversation. (excerpt)

—*Crystal D.*

What It Sounds Like at Night

In the night I hear crickets cracking. I also hear owls howling in the night and trying to catch mice and other animals. I hear frogs' tongues slashing in the night. I hear footsteps in the night. I hear thunder in the night. (excerpt)

—*James D.*

The night is dark the night has a moon and stars. I heard crickets in the night singing a song and I sing with them but then they get me all confused so I sing any song I think of.

—*Kristy C.*

I am utterly charmed by the idea of Kristy trying to sing along with the crickets while Crystal has a conversation ("confersashun" in her original text) with the peepers and James hides in bushes where he can hear the frogs slashing their tongues.

It's a wonder any of us got any sleep.

Seeing into the Hearts of Things

The poetry of children and of primitive peoples has much in common. Both are magical in that they seek to capture the essential spirit of something outside language, with a charged net of words. Vivid images, metaphor, rhythm, rhyme, and other sound devices, deeply felt symbols, and personification all play a part. The fact that these devices are not used consciously but rise from the emotional/nonintellectual mind only adds to their power.

A sophisticated, adult poet might be able to abstract and consciously manipulate the various plastic elements of a poem to gain an intellectually chosen effect. On the one hand, it is admirable to make art flow forth from artifice. On the other hand, perhaps we adults are only attempting, by means of our constantly growing intellects, to return to the sense of powerful magic that is in fact the primary impulse in the making of language at its origin.

When Janelle thinks about the night, in the following poem, she knows it is a thing of its own. Yet in it, she sees an owl; an appropriate choice, as the owl is the hunter of the night.

> I pretend the night is a huge black owl.
> The breeze you hear at night is the owl's big wings passing through.
> The other noises you hear is the owl's call.
> The screams you hear in the night is the owl chasing its prey.
> The light you see come through your window is the owl's bright yellow eyes.
> You think you hear thunder but it's the owl's wing knocking on the window.
> The owl's personality is to be proud that he is seen all around the world.
> You think you see lightning but it's the owl's yellow feet passing through.
>
> —*Janelle C.*

In her first line Janelle offers an owl as a symbolic substitute for the night. Her choice is perfect; she finds absolute identification between their various parts. The fact that the identification is absolute and not approximate is felt by her instinctive use of metaphor rather than simile. But she does something further; by the end of the poem, the symbol of the owl has superceded the thing it symbolizes. In the first line, she "pretends" the night is an owl. This pretending casts the night as the "real" subject and the owl as a secondary or substitute one. But immediately, there is a one-to-one equivalency between the two. The breeze is the same as and interchangeable with the owl's flapping wings; the light that enters your window (note the poet's natural and unconscious address to the reader) is the same as and interchangeable with the owl's bright yellow eyes. Then a subtle change occurs. You "think you hear thunder," but in fact, it's the owl's wings. The night becomes an image of and secondary to the owl, who is no longer the symbol but the essence. Then, a line that upon first reading may seem to be misplaced or inappropriate explains how it can be that the owl is now of greater importance than the night: he is seen all over the world. In his pride, the owl is able to replace the night. Given this context, the final image—"You think you see lightning but it's the owl's yellow feet passing through"—offers us clearly the poem's raison d'être; if the night is not the night, then the scary things in it, lightning and thunder, need not be feared. The owl may have the characteristics of night, but is essentially benign. This poem then, is ultimately a chant against the fear of the dark, of aloneness, of danger. When fear is cast into a familiar form, it becomes manageable.

The meditation I used with Janelle's class was on trying to get inside the spirit of something not living. We talked about all kinds of natural objects and phenomena—waterfalls, the moon, stars, a cyclone, a stone, a fossil, a cave. They listened with intense concentration as I suggested that a rock might have a spirit inside, that the wind can be the wind but also be like something else that is alive and familiar. It's important that you, as teacher, do no more than suggest the possibility of life in the inanimate and inexpressive. This possibility is not at all farfetched to a young child who has not yet forgotten all things exist in relationship to one another. You needn't suggest possibilities for whom the rock essentially is. Someone will immediately see how a rock is pretty much the same as a truck driver he knows, while someone else will see it as a quiet, blind grandmother who sits in her chair in the sun. Children are, to a large degree, tuned in. They can see into the hearts of things.

Before I Was Born

Preschoolers delight in spending hours being an animal or a flower. Sometimes they become something that completely lacks a physical body, or has one entirely and constantly mutable, such as a snowstorm or the wind. I knew a four-year-old kid who firmly believed he was a tornado, based on a chance innocent (and long-regretted) remark on the part of his mother after he had passed rapidly through the front door, up the stairs, into his room, and back down. He seemed to think there was no point in fighting his nature, and so he indulged in cyclonic behavior wherever he went. It was great, as far as he was concerned—a built-in excuse. Once, after having left the bathroom in several inches of soapy water, he shrugged and said to no one in particular, "Well, what do you expect from a cyclone?"

Young, school-aged children might have reached a point of sophistication at which they no longer really believe they are in truth a rabbit or a tuba, but they remember and like the game of pretending. In young classes, the kids and I sometimes talk about how we feel like something that isn't a human being. Lacey, author of the following piece, is petite and blond, a sunny little girl whose sweetness infects the other children so that they buzz around her. If in the piece she lets the others take her pollen for honey, in return she is blessed with their company:

> Before I was born I was a daffodil. In the field. In the summer. Sitting in the sun. It was really hot outside. I was yellow. Lots of bees hanged

around me. The field I was in was very big. I was the only flower there. I was very lonely. The bees take my pollen and make honey with it. Only the bees keep me company.

—*Lacey P.*

Like Janelle, Lacey seeks the mysterious internal life that is obscured by our everyday, human existence.

Standing in Place

While I think it's healthy, fun, and productive to allow and encourage kids to explore the wildest realms of imagination through games, meditation, and daydreaming, their journeys, lacking substance, will rapidly blow away unless they are firmly rooted to place. Some realistic observations will help both the writer and her audience grab hold of the experience. In order to help your writers locate grounding details in the worlds that exist only in their minds, give them plenty of external world experience. A meditation on a secret place, a hiding place, a place you were in once only, the darkest part of the house, or any other location will yield surprising results:

The Place Under the Waterfall

In the spring me & my Mom like to go up to the waterfall on our property. I have some secret rock stairs & two rock slides. On the ground is a lot of leaves & moss. Sometimes I find lizards on the ground near the trees. I also have a stream that has a whole bunch of frogs in it. My mom says I'm so fast and healthy because I've only got hurt on the rocks two times. All I do is jump from one rock to another. I've had a lot of experience up there. I like to go up to the very top of the waterfall and look down, down, down . . . . In the summer we can go swimming in the dock. Before my cat got run over she used to go up to the stream with me.

—*Chelsea H.*

There was a farm and I could hear the tractor running and it grumbled and there were some pigs, horses, cats, dogs, chicks, chickens, roosters and there was no grass under me just soil and then I went into all of the animals' pens and the last one I went to was the chicken coop and I saw some chicks all huddled up in a corner and you see when the big rooster crowed and they got scared so that's why they were all huddled up in a corner and then I reached down and picked them up one by one and their feet hurt my hand and they made it bleed a little and then when I reached down to pick up the last one . . . and it was in my hand I held it up to my face and it pinched my nose and I decided to take it home with me . . . . I showed my parents and then I went around to each house and when I got done I asked our carpenter to make a crate for my little chick . . . .

—Abra D.

Sharing

Soon after a child first makes symbols on a page, she will want to share. It is important that you allow a little bit of time at the end of your writing period for sharing. Sharing is important for a lot of reasons, some obvious, others less so:

- ❧ Confidence: A writer who shares work feels herself to be "a writer." The more she proves it by showing others what she has made, the more confident she becomes in the role. A confident writer is more willing to explore the intricacies of language, both written and spoken, to expand her mental horizon, and to extend herself into the world of experience in search of new material.

- ❧ Courage: The more you write and share it with other people, the more turned on you get. The more turned on you get, the more you can't wait to write and share some more. The more you write, propelled by sharing, the more competent you become at shaping letters, sound-letter association, blends, etc.

- ❧ Good Group Energy: Allows a transition from individual and private activity back to the community of the classroom.

- ❧ Generation of New Ideas: The more sharing that takes place in a classroom, the more the community members realize their choices in writing material and style are unlimited, and the more vivid becomes the imagination.

- ❧ Reward: Writers write to express themselves, and writing is satisfying in that alone. But writers also write to be read. Writing allows a bridging of the gap from one interior to another, and children feel the magic and power of this. Writing is its own reward, but sharing is also writing's reward.

However—no kid should ever be forced to share written work out loud. It's a matter of respect. Some kids are shy. Trying to help them over it by making them face it before they are ready can only lead to misery, theirs and yours. They will eventually leap over the barriers of shyness when they feel what they have written is sufficiently urgent. They must feel this from within; you can't feel it for them. Maybe it would be "good for them" to share, but if it's forced by you, it isn't sharing, and therefore, it isn't good for them.

Don't worry; for the most part, with a lot of cheering, balloons, and streamers tossed by you (in a pinch, I could mean this literally), kids will be willing and eager to share, even the ones you think never will. I have many, many times had teachers tell me "She doesn't like to read out loud," or "He thinks he can't read; he won't even try," only to have the he or she in question leap eagerly up and belt out a poem so lovely and pure it makes your heart stop.

Sharing can be done in several ways. You can simply ask, "Who wants to read?" If they are reluctant, embarrassed, or insecure, you can offer (the first few days) to read for them. A shy child might need you to act as "voice" longer than a more secure kid. But be careful they don't take advantage of you and rip themselves off by asking you to read their work aloud long into the school year. Reading for themselves really does have its own juice, and in addition, it reinforces reading skills. You can go around the room in some kind of order and ask each kid to read, but respect someone who doesn't want to. You can pick a reader, who then picks a reader, who then picks the next, turning it into a game. Of course, someone can be picked who decides to pass. Small sharing circles can be a good idea, if your kids work well together. Grouping five or six kids together to read what they wrote out loud can cover a lot of territory quickly.

Sharing can also be done nonverbally. It's important to hang work in a highly visible place. You might want to display final drafts in the hall, works in progress at kid-eye level around the classroom. You can also have a library corner, where final drafts that have been written into a book are available to read, or even to check out.

Finally, a child who is particularly involved with writing should be encouraged to share with other classrooms. You might want to work out a writer-in-residency exchange program with the teacher next door, or ask the younger grades if they would like to have a reader come to share a story or a poem.

Ma, I Wanna Be a Star

Have a poetry reading at least once in the school year. This should be a very big deal event. It can be in the classroom or in the auditorium, during school, after school, or in the evening. Punch is a must, and cookies and fruit and fancy napkins and confetti and nice taped music—classical adds an elegant touch, but some kids would rather rock and roll. Get a grown-up to don a tux with tails and offer peanut butter cookies off a silver tray; or get several grown-ups to dress as characters from Alice in Wonderland, or even as characters from a group story. A printed program is very, very nice, and can be done pretty easily on the school computer. If you really want to make a project out of it, you can print the texts that will be read. This is especially helpful in that some kids will duck their heads, others will mumble, others will read their poem at warp speed. Invite the press. No kidding. Get someone with a video recorder to save the event for posterity. And you read something, too.

4

Third Grade: Grooving Along

When a Thousand Words Isn't Worth One Lousy Picture

Adults sometimes get tangled up in saying nothing in a fancy way because they think it makes them sound particularly business-wise or irreproachably intelligent. It works, too. Everyone is very impressed. And very intimidated. Whether it is a memo from the boss, a statement from a politician, or even directions for assembling a new toy, the message is too often lost. Specialized language, whether of a business, political, religious, or social nature, is clear only to the inner circle who have learned or earned their way in. It can be used to:

- Impress outsiders
- Identify peers from out of the masses
- Communicate secret or privy information
- Cover the fact that what you are saying is boring
- Cover the fact that you don't know what it is you're saying, exactly, but that you hope someone else does and will tip you off

Outsiders might be dazzled, but it would never occur to them to charge the fortress and demand a drawbridge of clarity be lowered.

But imageless language, heavily specialized vocabulary, and syntax twisted to the point of pain are useless if what you're trying to do is write something vivid enough to leap off the page and jump into the reader's lap. Oftentimes, writers overload a story with wordy words, in hopes that the reader will be impressed enough not to look beyond the fancy surface for the deeper meaning that is missing.

Kids have their own version of this message-obscuring technique. It goes something like this:

> Yesterday I had a great time. My friends and I played. We had fun, a lot of fun. A lot, lot, lot of fun. It was great! My mom gave us a snack, we liked it a lot. It was really good. My mom is nice usually. Sometimes she's not nice. But usually she's nice. She said my friends could sleep over. They did, and we really had fun!!!!!

In the above un-story, there are only three real pieces of information:

1. My friends came over yesterday.
2. We got a snack.
3. They stayed overnight.

According to the dictionary, to *inform* means "to give form to, to animate." Look up *animate* and you discover it means "to give spirit or life to something." Only three jolts of life, only three spiritual moments in the above piece of writing. That's it; the rest is nothing but empty skins that rustle when you wade through them looking for the flesh.

I presented the first version to a plugged-in group of third graders. We talked at great length about what was wrong with it. They knew right off the bat it was boring. Why was it boring? Because it isn't interesting. Ho, hum, what do you mean? Because it isn't saying anything about what happened! Little by little, we studied the words on the board to try to find an interesting, unboring, even exciting story behind the meaningless construct of words:

> Yesterday my friend Amanda came over to my house with her sister, Tara. We draped sheets from the ceiling and made my room into a big tent. The sheets smelled like lemon when the wind billowed them. We sprawled under the tent and pretended we were nomads. We found a cave under the desk for the camels to sleep. My bed blossomed into an oasis. My mom brought us a coconut and some chewy dried fruit that felt like leather. She stuck straws in the coconut so we could drink the juice, because it was hot in the desert. She put on a jingling belt made out of coins and pretended to be a dancing girl, but when she spinned around, she spotted her best sheets hanging from my ceiling. She yelled so loud we got scared and Tara cried. Then she was sorry and we were sorry. She muttered, Well,

since the sheets are up, you can stay overnight and sleep in the tent.
We slept on the floor in our blankets.

From Vague Language to Clear Image

Details

Rewriting the above un-story into a dynamic, vivid piece took a lot of
work. The first thing we did was circle all the words that didn't give us a
picture:

> Yesterday I had a *great time*. My friends and I played. We had *fun, a
> lot of fun. A lot, lot, lot of fun. It was great!* My mom gave us a snack, we
> *liked it a lot. It was really good.* My mom is *nice usually. Sometimes* she's
> not *nice.* But *usually* she's *nice.* She said my friends could sleep over.
> They did, and we *really had fun*!!!!!

That was most of the story. We decided what was missing were the real
details of what could have happened. "There's lots of different great
times," one kid mused; "I can't picture the story if I don't know which
great time you mean." The kids had many questions:

> Who were the friends?   Where did you play?   What
> did you play?   What did you have for a snack? Why
> did your mother get mad?   Why did she let your
> friends stay overnight?   Where did you all sleep?

After they listed the questions, they began to piece together answers.

Using the Senses

After they had posed questions about the narrative line of the story, we
talked about the five senses. I have stressed the importance of asking
meditating writers to experience their visions fully by looking for all kinds
of sensory detail. This is as true of first graders as it is of full-grown,
professional writers. We know the world through our experience of it, and
our experience of it comes from our bodies, specifically, from our senses.
The story came alive as the writers added details of touch, smell, and
sound. The sheets began to billow in a breeze that smelled like lemons (no
doubt, from Mom's laundry soap, but how appropriate for setting the
scene for the story). The dried fruit was chewy in the mouth and felt like
leather. Underneath the desk it was cool, like a cave, but out in the room

it was desert hot. When the mother donned the belt and danced, we heard a jingling, but she had the capacity as well to yell and scare everybody.

Be Specific

A good story or poem makes pictures. Words that are specific are full of information (life) and meaning and allow the mind to see a much fuller picture. Writers use specific words whenever they can; writers seek the spirits of things through words, and are therefore always seeking the word with the correct spirit.

According to the poet W. C. Williams, each object in nature and each idea has an exact name. In my mind, this means the poet must seek, with great determination, the image and then the exact word or words that contain and communicate that image.

Many words are very broad in meaning and therefore, nonspecific; they name instead a group of things. If you pay attention to your daily conversations, you will discover that you and everyone else tend to use these nonspecific, nonimagistic words with far greater frequency. There is a practical reason for this. When we speak to one another, we are referring to and relying upon the environment we occupy to provide the context. It would sound and, indeed be silly to ask your husband to put the spotted dachsund puppy outside the red patio door. He knows the dog's got spots, he knows the door is red and he knows the patio door is the one the dog always goes out of. Instead, you abbreviate the verbal message to: "Hey, sweetie, stick the dog out."

But poetry uses *itself* as its total context. A reader cannot (reasonably) get out of a poem any more than is in it in the first place, unless she is making assumptions, or allowing the images or the language to kick off her own memories and imagination. And the truth is, readers are of only two minds—already bored or wildly imaginative. A poet who loves her vision and wants it to be understood, will carefully guard against both these extremes. Using the exact word(s) to convey a vision of clarity will trigger excitement, not boredom, in any reader. At the same time, the exact word is the author's means of establishing and maintaining control. Your reader cannot go zipping off in the wrong direction entirely if you call him to heel via your carefully, exactly chosen words.

Discuss the difference between specific words and general words with your class. Choose two words and ask them which is more specific:

armadillo	animal
gum	Bubblicious

knife	switchblade
bonnet	hat
slipper	shoe

The specific word is always the one that provides more information and a better visual picture. After they have selected the more specific of the pair, demand a host of other specific examples of a general category. For example, a utensil can be:

a soup spoon   a silver spoon   a fork   chopsticks
fingers   a bread knife   a wooden spoon   an egg-
beater   a butter knife   a honey dipper

Once the difference between nonspecific, imageless words and specific, picture words has been established, give the kids a bland statement and let them jazz it up: "I have a new piece of clothing."

Ask them to imagine the clothing in all its glorious detail, then select which of the details to write down and in what words. Some of the kids will also spend time on the verb *have*, replacing it with *borrowed, bought, found, stole, discovered, saw, won.*

Dancing Verbs

Just as there are "true" names for things, there are names for activities that embody a particular spirit. Anybody knows a verb names an action, a motion, but think about this: How do you slow down an action long enough to name it?

Obviously the best you can do is grab its spirit for a second, slap a label on what palpitates in your hands, and hope your meaning comes clear. Some verbs are used so frequently they cover a whole spectrum of qualities. To walk really means to *stumble, amble, stagger, limp, creep, tippy-toe, stomp, drag, hop, shimmy, strut, wobble, wiggle, crawl, slither,* or *bop.* You can sit in a chair, but I can't see it as well as I can picture you sprawling, slouching, leaning, coiling, hunkering, or splaying. A specific verb is stronger than a verb+adverb combination. To walk quickly is to trot, to walk slowly is to stroll or amble.

Name Tags

The right name for a thing calls a picture into the mind, and for that, it is a piece of magic. A name that is too big, too much a category, gives no clear picture because there are too many possibilities. It functions more as a place holder than anything. "Somebody gave me flowers for my birthday" is a nice statement, but I'm not going to get nearly as excited by it as I will if you tell me, "My husband gave me a bouquet of lilies, baby's breath, and baby pink roses"; or "The neighbor kid picked a handful of dandelions for me on my birthday"; or "Auntie Eunice gave me some dusty plastic sunflowers for my garden on my birthday." Each statement is true in terms of "somebody gave me a flower for my birthday," but each statement goes beyond a simple truth. Each offers a vivid image, a picture for the mind to hold on to and believe in.

Getting Down

Look again at the rewrite of the story I gave my third-grade gang. The board was gorgeous by the time we were finished. I had left a lot of room between words and between lines. As we made changes I wrote them in. Someone had me write "put sheets around the room"; someone else suggested the sheets "smelled nice and clean when the wind blew." I had to push hard and insist that there was a better picture that could be made. They came up eventually with the fact that the sheets weren't just "around the room": that could give entirely the wrong picture. They actually (in the actual place of our minds) were on the ceiling. They didn't just smell good, they smelled exactly like Fab, which smelled like lemons. And the most beautiful of all, the wind didn't simply blow, it billowed the sheets! Push hard, but never stop enjoying the gaming aspect; remember, this is fun, it's a challenge, it's a game. With that attitude, the kids will get right in there with you.

To summarize, ingrain these few absolutely urgent concepts into the minds of your flock:

- ✎ Good writing uses specific verbs and nouns to make pictures, or images. If you want someone to know what you mean, tell him what you mean.
- ✎ Good writing gives enough details.
- ✎ Remember to always use your five senses when telling a story.
- ✎ Keep as far away from vague words as possible; they are death to the spirit of the story.

Folktales

Third graders love folktales as much as second graders, and their increasing vocabulary, experience, and mental sophistication can result in delightful stories to share out loud. Because they substitute objects with human personalities for human characters, folktales allow kids to tackle some of the difficult problems and issues that confront them in a non-threatening and symbolically satisfying way. Jealousy, feelings of competition, guilt over increasing independence, insecurity, and so on all provide thematic substance to third-grade-created folktales.

You can use any natural setting (or even any man-made setting, without the people present) as the beginning for a folktale. A creek with a bridge, rocks, an insect, and a bent tin can will work as well as the sky with its pantheon of characters—sun, moon, stars, clouds, bird, lightning, and so forth.

The Day the Sun and Moon Had a Fight

One sunny day, when the moon was sleeping and the sun was babysitting the moon's little star children (for stars never go to sleep, they only take one nap in the day), the sun was exercising to make heat and let the children play. So the stars played. But one problem. They made too much noise and that woke their mother up. The moon was angry. She got up and told the children to play quietly. Now the sun didn't know that and thought something was wrong. When he turned around he saw the moon. Angry. "You nut," she said, not so loud because she is a quiet moon. "You let my children play and didn't tell them to be quiet." The sun said "they should know to be quiet by now, besides, you are the one responsible for your children." The moon said, "they're only little and need to be reminded and you're responsible for them when I'm sleeping."

They argued and argued until the moon took her children home and they all had to go to sleep. Now the wise owl heard all this and knew what had happened. "This cannot go on." he said. He flew up into the sky, very quietly woke up all the stars, which was easy because they weren't tired. "The sun and your mother are very angry at each other," he said. "Why don't half of you talk to your mother about it and half of you talk to the sun about it. Tell them how you care. After about 25 minutes, switch. So all of you can talk to the sun and your mother. Now if they tell you to go away or they don't want to talk about it don't go if you want them to come back as friends. After about 23 minutes, go and let them think about it."

The stars did as the owl had said and it worked. The next day the sun went to see the moon and they both apologized. Then they lived happy, friendly, quiet in the day, ever after.

—*Mary V.*

Additional Fiction-Writing Ideas

Third graders are at a pleasant point in their lives; they have struggled and scrambled up the rocky sides of the steep cliff of language and experience and have reached a resting place. They have a zillion ideas of their own to explore in the making of stories, with a little bit of help from you. They will delight in meditations based on wildly giddy fantasies as well as those firmly grounded in the reality of experience and memory. Remember, however, that good story writing has behind it a committed author who is serious about his work. Fantasy stories about green monsters who are seventeen thousand feet tall and have six zillion heads lack . . . well . . . integrity. You know the writer didn't really visualize this particular monster, and so why should you, as a reader, believe it?

Most of the story ideas I suggest for fourth and fifth graders can be tailored for your third-grade writers. Read the chapter and choose those you think they would get juiced by—and ask them for ideas as well. You might want to keep a big, handmade book listing story ideas someplace in your classroom. Anyone can contribute to it at any time, and you can use those occasional spare moments while waiting for the bus call or when everyone (for once) gets work done early, to brainstorm as a group.

Poetry

For several years, I didn't teach poetry to kids. Why? Well, because I was scared. I knew how to write the stuff, and I knew how to teach, but I didn't think I knew how to teach them to write the stuff. While a great many of my children wrote in the form I expected would be easiest and most natural—prose—there were always a few kids in each class who would shape their words, which were particularly succinct, into lines, and their lines into stanzas: in short, there were always some poets.

Now, that was fine with me, except that I didn't see any point in urging the rest of the group to try their hand at it. Plus, I felt as stuck as the teachers who would come to me after class and ask, "How can we teach them to write poetry?" If I failed with people as young as eight or nine years old, then everyone would think I was a sham and I would lose my job, my apartment, my friends, my savings account, and the respect of my family, in rapidly descending order.

Besides, fiction I was more sure of. All of us spend at least part of our time telling stories to one another—gossip, fish tales, old wives' tales, anecdotes relayed at the Grand Union while waiting for the checkout girls to finish exchanging their bits of stories about last Friday night and who broke up with whom. Stories are easy. You just reach into your life or someone else's any old place, figure out the words that go with the life, and start writing. You can stretch truths, lie a little or a lot, rearrange time sequences, or overlap two separate events. See? Easy.

Then a horrible thing happened. Midway through a residency in a particular class, a boy who had consistently shaped his writing into long narrative poems approached me. "I want to know about poems," he said. "I like to write them and I don't know why. I know they're different but I don't know how. Can we do poems tomorrow?" My heart started to punch like a fist. In truth I didn't know if I could give the boy what he wanted—some direction, some explanation, some intelligent encouragement that would lead him toward his own discovery of poetry. Teachers who ask me to help their kids write poetry share my belief that poetry *is* different than prose. But how is it different, and how do the differences work in contributing toward the total meaning of the poem, and how can the writer control the ways language works in a poem that is different from the way language works in daily communication?

After I got done whimpering, I decided to do the only sensible thing. I would ask the kids to search for the answers with me. I would not ask them coyly or condescendingly, not ask them as a trick to get them to apply themselves, but really, sincerely ask them to help me understand how much it is they are capable of understanding about poetry.

Bingo. By the end of the next day, it felt as though my toes were skimming the surface of the earth. I not only realized I could teach poetry, and that they could write poetry, true poetry that was different from prose; I realized something I had been in danger of forgetting: we teach each other, we always do. That's what living as a human being has always been about. It's a passing back and forth of knowledge, clear vision, patterns of understanding, and sudden insights. Nobody has all the answers all the time, and nobody has none of the answers all the time.

That morning, when I arrived in the classroom, I asked to see a show of hands as to how many were interested in doing some poetry. Nearly every hand went up. I told them I wasn't sure how to teach poetry writing. We began by making a list on the board about the nature of stories and what we knew:

- **They have people in them (characters).**
- **Something happens.**
- **They take place someplace.**

- They can be about something that could happen (realism).
- They can be about something that couldn't happen (fantasy).
- They can have chapters.
- They use specific verbs and nouns to make a picture (image).
- Lots of details help you see what the story is about.
- You should use your five senses when writing a story.

I wrote the word POETRY next to our list and waited, chalk hovering. Nothing. Not a squeak. Finally, I heard a throat clearing. I turned around to see my poet of the day before cautiously lifting his hand.

"They rhyme?" he asked. That was interesting, because the poems he had written during my residency didn't have a single rhyme in them. But the rest of the class seemed to agree. A lot of nodding heads in response to this one. I wrote *rhyme* on the board.

"Okay," I said, "if we're going to really figure out the difference between poetry and fiction, we have to look deep into every word we use. What does *rhyme* mean? What does *rhyme* have to do with?"

"Two words that rhyme sound alike on the end," a little boy in a Mohawk haircut chanted. Again, nodding heads.

"Examples?" I asked. After a minute to think, they started pouring in: cat/hat/bat/fat; pink/ink/sink/fink; disappear/pioneer; chair/hair.

"Anybody have any they aren't sure about?" I asked, after the flood of rhymes had abated.

A hesitant hand lifted slightly, dropped, floated up again, and hovered. "Nest and next?" its owner asked.

Before I could begin to think about that, someone else said, "Fair and fear?"

"Tarp and warp?" queried a third. That one brought laughter. I wrote them on the board so the class could see why there might be a question as to whether they rhymed.

"Oh," said a fourth, "they do rhyme, but in my eye, not in my ear."

I stopped them there. "Okay," I said, "do nest and next, fear and fair rhyme? What do they have to do with?"

"Sound," came the response from several mouths at once. "They don't rhyme, but they do sound alike."

"And they'd be good in a poem. Poems have a lot of sound in them." someone added.

I wrote SOUND above *rhyme*. An argument broke out at that point. A little guy with aviator glasses pointed out that all words have sound. Someone else said, yeah, but in poems especially. Things were getting pretty heated; literary theory always has this effect; it's worse than politics for getting spleen up.

"Hold it," I said. "What other sounds besides end sounds can be the same in two words?"

As the kids thought about it and came up with answers, I jotted them on the board. Pretty soon, we had accumulated a pretty comprehensive list:

- **Beginning sounds (banana/bicycle)**
- **Middle sounds (bat/can)**
- **End sounds (pat/cut)**
- **The beginning of one word and the middle or end of another word (elephant/laughter)**
- **Two words with similar but different sounds (nest/next)**

"So, do poems *have* to have rhyme?"

A few heads shook up and down. A few shook side to side. Several of them wobbled slightly in bewilderment, like newly hatched birds.

"No," somebody said. "But they do have to have sounds."

At this point, the tarp/warp kid raised his hand and firmly added, "They have to have sounds or sights. Maybe there's a poem that rhymes when you read it but not when you hear it."

"What are some other things you know about poems?"

"They're shorter. Stories can go on for pages and pages and pages, but poems usually don't."

"But they can," a stickler for accuracy interjected.

"But they usually don't," my little teacher persisted firmly.

I urged them to think about what it means if the poem is shorter. They came up with a lot of repercussions. You had to leave a lot out, you couldn't include as many words, so the ones to use must be very well chosen. A story might be about things happening to people, whereas a poem might not be about anything happening, and it might not even have a person in it.

"So, if you write something that doesn't have people and isn't about a happening, what could it be about?"

"Feelings," a kid in a red-and-pink-dotted visor cap promptly said.

"You mean like, 'Oh, I feel so good, la la la, I feel like laughing not crying but laughing I'm so happeeeeeee!?'" I asked.

Absolutely not, the class decided. A lousy poem indeed. "And why is it a lousy poem?"

"It doesn't make a single picture."

"It doesn't have good sounds. It isn't rhyming or making sounds that are like other words."

"You didn't tell me why you're happy, you didn't tell me why you wanted to laugh, you didn't even tell me who you were!"

The girl with the hat looked very, very thoughtful. She chewed the end of one braid, then another. "I don't mean it talks about *your* feeling," she said at last. "I mean ... I mean ... oh, what do I mean?" I held my breath. "I mean," she said very slowly, moving through her thoughts so cautiously they wouldn't scamper off before she could capture them in a net of words, "I mean that it makes a feeling inside me when I read it."

A poem makes a feeling inside me when I read it. That's as satisfying and sophisticated a definition of poetry I have ever come across. Good poetry is never sentimental; it doesn't simply talk about the narrator's emotional state. It calls out for an emotional, even spiritual response in the reader, one that rises out of the words but is more than just the sum total of the words' meanings.

A poem is shorter than a story. Its words must be especially well chosen. It is often about an image or a mood, an atmosphere. It pays attention to the sounds of its words, although it doesn't have to rhyme. What else?

"Looks different." This observation was from the class tough guy. He crossed his arms on his chest. "Got a shape," he added grandly, in case I missed the point.

I wrote SHAPE on the board. "Shape," I read back to them. "Where does the shape come from?"

Well, that was obvious: it comes from the poet. I said to them, "Okay, you're all poets because today you're going to write poems. So, where does the shape come from?"

"It's on the paper," a hesitant soul offered.

"Sure is, and where did it come from?"

"Because you stop every time you find a rhyme?" someone queried.

"Yeah, but many, many poems don't have rhymes in them."

"Poet's brain," the tough guy said firmly. Several kids nodded.

"From the poem," the boy who wanted to write poetry disagreed, just as firmly. I fervently wished Helen Elam, with whom I had studied literary theory, was here to listen to and guide this discussion.

"Why?" I asked either one. "What makes you say that?"

There was a very long and meditative pause. Finally, the tough guy shrugged and grinned impishly. "Because," he drawled, "I am a poet and I write poems and I say where the shape comes from."

The poetic soul rolled his eyes, beseeching the gods for support. "Well, I'm a poet too, and I write poems too, and the shape gets put the way it gets put because it just should!"

These are two pretty sophisticated positions, each implying a complex and interesting set of assumptions.

To the tough guy, the artist is the craftsperson/god in utter control of his vision and material. The art object comes strictly through his making, and he does not need to be concerned with a preordained aesthetic handed to him from his culture, his religion, or even his biology. To him, the artist either has the power and ability to leap beyond an other-imposed aesthetic. Or it is already so deeply ingrained in him that how he chooses to shape the poem will fulfill the needs of the inherited aesthetic without interfering with his full and individual vision.

To the poetic soul, the artist is the conduit through which the poem, a thing unto itself, passes. He has literally been inspired, has breathed in the vision, which has a life and an impulse beyond his own. Just as he has "inhaled" it from the cosmos, he must "exhale" it onto the paper, being utterly sensitive to the shape the poem requires, and ideally, *is*.

Far be it from me to suggest there is a correct or incorrect position in all of this. I merely give it to you to illustrate the sophistication of young children's thinking about philosophical issues that have fascinated and perturbed their elders forever. More importantly, I want to show you the passion with which young kids approach the making of a poem. They need to feel that the poem is organic, that they make or discover its shape because of their relationship to the words and the images.

So, How Do You Teach Line Breaks?

We've already established that a poem is different from a piece of fiction. For one thing, a poem has a shape, as my tough-guy writer said. The shape is determined by how the lines in the poem are broken on the page. Kids from third grade up are able to consider the question of line breaks quite thoroughly. If you ask them, "How do you know where to break the line?" you will get at least some of the following answers:

> at the end of a sentence
> wherever you find a comma

wherever you get a new picture
when you find a whole new idea
wherever you feel like it
when you stop to take a breath
where you want to make a certain shape

The first two possibilities seem, at first glance, to be based on the rules of grammar and not on any sensitivity on the part of the poet. However, remember that a third-grade writer is much more attuned to the actual function of a comma or period than you or I. Punctuation is nothing more than a convenience, used solely in writing. We don't punctuate in our spoken communications to one another; we don't need to. We can pause to emphasize a point or to suggest we are going on to the next idea. We can turn our backs slightly to indicate we are going to stop talking soon and leave the room. We can pitch our voices high with excitement and wave our arms. We can lilt the tail end of a stream of words to show our culturally attuned listener we are asking a question. These things are expressed in speech by cadence, silence, and emphasis. All punctuation is, is cadence, silence and emphasis in a visually symbolic form. What is a period, but a slightly turned back? A comma, but a pause to swallow? A question mark, but the indication in the reader's mind of a gently lilting voice? So when a third grader realizes that you can stop one line of poetry when you arrive at a period or a comma, he is really telling you that a pause in the linguistic flow can be symbolically underscored by leaving one line and beginning another.

A kid who can tell you to stop one line and begin another each time you have a new picture or image in your mind, has learned well. He is using line breaks to organize time. It's as if he has a stack of photographs taken at a party. One by one he studies the photos for details, for information, for meaning. One by one, he puts them aside and goes on to the next. Some photos he will dwell on because they are especially evocative or because there is so much to look at. Some photos will slip by with little more than a glance. It doesn't matter if the busy photo took no longer to snap than the less evocative ones. Recollected moments, whether they are located in a photo album or in a poem, often distort the original flow of time.

Breaking lines of poetry "wherever you feel like it" depends both on the writer's sense of himself as utterly powerful, and as utterly intuitive. I love this answer, it's so gutsy and so simple at the same time. It conjures in my mind the symbol ☯, the Taoist symbol for the two elemental and essential principles of energy upon which all life is based. Yin is essentially receptive, fertile, accepting, soft, yielding, mysterious, female, and intuitive. Yang is essentially aggressive, powerful, outward moving, hard, urgent, strong, male, and decisive. Everyone, man and woman, has both energies within. Certain situations bring out your yin, others, your yang. "Wherever you feel like it" indicates both the power and control of the writer, and the writer's willingness to feel intuitively where the lines should be broken.

Some kids are hip to breaking the line "whenever you stop to take a breath," although this answer eludes most young writers. This is not that far removed from breaking the line "whenever you reach a comma," except it's both a little more emotional and a little more biological. You might stop to take a breath just before you shout something, or you might stop to breathe after you've said something that makes you sigh and get all wispy for a moment.

As for breaking the line "where you want to make a certain shape": kids are very alert to the way the poem's shape contributes subtly and nonverbally to the overall meaning. I strongly recommend you find a book on concrete poetry for your class shelves that contains concrete poems, whose meanings are utterly part and parcel with the forms. Kids love these, because they so wonderfully marry the idea of visual art with the idea of verbal art. Really explore concrete poetry with them, maybe include the art teacher in a project. One word of caution, however: do not expose them to concrete poetry until well into the school year, after they have become comfortable with writing poetry in which the lines are broken not solely or primarily for their visual effect. Some kids are so excited by concrete poetry once they are exposed to it they get the mistaken notion that all poetry should appear as concrete poetry.

Class Act

"Let's do a poem together to see if we can figure out this line-break business. Who is it about?"

"Oh! My sister!"

"Okay, how old is she?"

"Sixteen."

"What does a sixteen-year-old sister look like?"

"His sister is skinny; I've seen her."

"What else?"

"Long yellow hair and a phone stuck in her mouth."
"More."
"Tells other people's secrets on the phone."
"Yeah, she gossips."
"Eats pizza, ice cream, and Coke, then talks about getting fat."
"More."
"Sits on the bed."
"How?"
"Curls up like a cat."
"Slouches."
"Sprawls, because she's skinny. She wouldn't curl up."
"Yeah, with the phone. And kicks her feet in the air and giggles."
"Put it all together and tell me what to write."

> My sister is skinny and has long yellow hair. She tells her friends secrets when she sprawls on the bed. She has pizza, ice cream, and Coke on the table. She talks about getting fat. She kicks her feet in the air and giggles.

"Put it in two sentences."
We study the board.
A lot of scribbling and erasing, crossing out, muttering. Finally:

> My skinny sister sprawls on the bed and kicks her feet while giggling on the phone about getting fat. She has pizza, ice cream, and Coke on the bedside table.

"Good. I like *sprawls, kicks, giggles*. What does she do with the food on the table?"
"Eats it."
"No, she doesn't. The pizza is cold, the ice cream is melted, the Coke is warm."
"She looks at it."
"Do! Do! What does she *do*!"
"Do?"
"Yup."
"She sticks her finger in the ice cream."
"Yeah, she doodles in her food!"
"Okay, I got it, write this: 'She doodles her finger in her melting ice cream while she talks.'"
"Talks? Got something better?"
"Oh, okay.—'while she gossips.'"

" No! I got it. 'She doodles her finger in melting ice cream and gossips other people's secrets'?"

As each correction or change occurred, I crossed out the previous version and wrote in the alteration. By the time the class was finished, we had the following:

> My skinny sister sprawls on the bed and kicks her feet while giggling
> on the phone about getting fat. She doodles her finger in melting ice
> cream and gossips other people's secrets.

Someone wanted to change *melting* to *gooey* because it sounded better. Upon questioning, he pointed out that *gooey* sounds like *doodle* in the middle. Someone else noticed that *gooey* also sounded like *gossips* initially.

After a long talk about line breaks in which we reviewed all the options, the class arrived at the following long, skinny shape, which was chosen because "it looks like my sister."

> My skinny sister
> sprawls
> across the bed
> and kicks
> her feet
> while
> giggling on the phone about getting fat.
> She doodles
> her finger
> in gooey ice cream
> and gossips
> other people's
> secrets.

There was quite a bit of discussion about that long line in the middle. Several kids were disturbed by it because it interrupted the skinny unfolding of the poem. However, one of the girls pointed out that line wasn't about being skinny, it was about being fat. The class decided the fat line was appropriate to the skinny girl's fear of becoming dumpy.

Stuff of Life

In the village of North Rose, there's a fat white rabbit who monitors the halls and is willing to escort you to the teacher's lounge or the lunchroom, with his long white ears flopping and waving like clean laundry. This school is great. The kids are interested in one another's efforts, they cheer each other on, and they have a kind of subtle yet zany sense of humor.

One day my third graders came shuffling into the room from their gym class. They looked as if their bodies had been sucked completely dry of blood. The whole class was subtly exaggerating their exhaustion. They zombied to their desks, draped themselves across the tops, and slid into their seats. No one said a word, just a lot of sighing and yawning. Now, you don't let a wonderful thing like this slip away unnoticed. I tossed aside the lesson I'd planned for the day, draped myself across the top of the teacher's desk, sighed, and snored. After I was sure I had their attention, I announced in my most exhausted voice, "Today we better write tired poems." Nods of approval. I yawned. They yawned. We stretched. I reminded them to use their senses, to use strong verbs and nouns. Here are two of the resulting poems:

Being Tired

When I'm
Tired it feels
Like my body is broken down.
My nose feels
Like its broken.
My head is drowsy,
My heart is dead
I have just been
Murdered.

—*Cory T.*

I walk in the
Blue room hanging like
a sleepy person that
can't get up
and I feel like
Drooping to the
floor and going
back to bed

—*Michelle D.*

Self-Portraits

Third graders like themselves, by and large. They like themselves a lot, and if they don't, they should. They like themselves as a group, and that helps them to like themselves as individuals. They are for the most part self-sufficient. They tend to their own problems and disagreements, they have learned to work things out without adult help or interference. When a third grader looks at himself, he sees someone who is greatly capable, living in a world in which other people take a back seat. Third graders love to meditate about themselves in a background dear to their various hearts, involved in something that just kind of says it all. A daredevil in yesterday's class wrote about dangling upside down off a willow branch while the little leaves danced against his face. A peaceful girl wrote about studying the goldfish's translucent tail that went through the water like a wind she couldn't feel!

I would like to stress the importance of the meditation when working with these kids, and with all kids. The meditation both offers the writers an inspired image from which to work and magically replaces the present with a past that is still vivid and alive. Note the use, in both these poems, of the present-tense verbs. During the meditation, suggest to your kids they are not in the present remembering, but in the past; what they remember is happening all over again, just as strongly as it did the first time.

3 Years Old

I am squatting in a room where
walls are brown.
My diaper is on.
My hair is in a ponytail.
I pick up my crayon and scribble on my
Winnie the Pooh coloring book all alone.
I scribble on almost all the pages.
I go and sit on the couch and listen to the
water running down the pipes of the kitchen.

—*Dayana K.*

Notice that by implementing present-tense verbs, Dayana does away with the need, and even the opportunity, of punctuating and puncturing her poem with a lot of "I remember"s. She carries us into the past with a strong and certain voice. Because she simply observes herself and fully informs us of what she observes, we are able to experience what is left unsaid. Note too that the very simplicity of the memory—the fact that it lacks the drama of a car wreck or a lost puppy—contributes to the strength and authenticity of the poet's voice.

Reading

Today is Sunday.
We just got the paper.
Every Sunday Jolana's
parents give the funnies
to Jolana to look at.
Jolana is three years old.
Jolana is looking at the
pictures, Jolana smells
breakfast on the stove.
All of a sudden Jolana's
parents hear "b-l-o-n-d-i-e
said g-o to the sch-o-o-l right
now!" And finally Jolana
was reading! And only
three years old! Jolana's
mom and dad are
very happy for Jolana.

—*Jolana D.*

In this poem too, the poet sees herself as terrifically independent and self-sufficient. Jolana sets the scene with a minimum of verbiage and just the right details: Sunday leads gracefully into the funnies, which leads to the baby Jolana looking at the pictures while Mom and Dad make breakfast. The fact that the narrator doesn't notice anyone doing the cooking, but only her own sensory attention to it ("Jolana smells breakfast on the stove") only helps further prepare the reader for the amazing event that is about to take place in this life of this remarkably independent child—her miraculous intellectual leap into reading!

I am particularly tickled by this writer's obvious pride and self-confidence as illustrated by the memory she holds of herself. In her mind, the baby Jolana had absolutely no problems overcoming the illogic of "sch" (school)—although she did have to spell out "o-o-l"! And *right*, pronounced phonetically, is a guttural groan; but the brilliant child Jolana lilts it effortlessly off the end of her tongue. I would also like to point out the control of the craft Jolana the writer exhibits in this poem. She retains the present tense throughout, except when the temporal scheme *framed by the poem* refers to a past that is within the poem ("And finally Jolana was reading!"). She does not at that point slip into the past tense for the remainder of the poem, which would have been a quite natural error to make, but returns to the present tense of the poem.

Camouflage

Third graders like to hide. I hold a secret belief that everybody likes to hide, even grown-ups; but third graders are still in the golden age of playfulness and they aren't afraid to admit it. They are like bats; they get into hiding places you or I wouldn't even imagine. Once I opened an antique jelly cabinet in which my friend kept an assortment of canned soup and boxed cereal. The shelves had been neatly cleared out, and wedged on the bottom shelf with his knees up his nose was an eight-year-old. I asked him what he was doing in there. He tried to turn his head to look at me, but he was jammed in too tightly. "Just thinking," he said. As good a place as any, I guess.

Outside Hiding Place

It is a light blue sky, cool spring day.
I feel like hiding.
Hiding in my secret hiding place,
Only me and my two friends know where
it is.
  It's behind my house.
  In my side yard, there is a fence dividing
up my neighbors' and my property.
    In one corner of my house,
  where the fence and that corner meet,
    there is a loose part of the fence.
    I can take it off,
    and go to the back of my house.
    I see bushes, birds, plants.
    I hear wind, birds' stomachs growling
    and then my mother calling me,
    for lunch.

—*Mary V.*

My guess is that it wasn't a bird's stomach growling that Mary heard, but her own, because in the next line her mother calls her to come and eat!

Note Mary's masterful handling of line breaks. She shapes the poem in such a way that the reader receives a precise verbal mapping of how to find her hiding place. She uses line breaks to pace us as well, moving us slowly through the poem just as she moves slowly through her yard.

The fact that she invites us to enter and share the secret of her hiding place privileges us, the readers, in the making of the poem. We feel we are being whispered to by her words, are being made special by being allowed to read the poem. This is a pretty clever thing for a poet of any age to do. By assuring us we are privileged and special, the poet increases her own power over us!

My Secret Hiding Place

My secret hiding place is inside a bush,
there's just a little space inside but it
certainly is a big bush.
The ground is always dirty.
It's like a little home as you
go in on the right is the kitchen
on the left my
bedroom,
and the little part that
separates it is the
front hall.
It's usually in the afternoon after my
lunch has filled me up.
It's usually when the sun is shining
bright, it's usually when those
bees are buzzing and get me dreadfully scared.
The things I can see
from where I sit, which is usually the front
hall. I can see the inside of the bush
the driveway and the tree next door.

—*Julia D.*

What I like about this piece is the attention she gives to letting her voice emerge. The rhythmic repetition of *usually* establishes an expectation in the reader's ear, and at the same time, each occurrence of the word focuses a lens more tightly on the temporal and spatial configurations of the hiding place. Julia is as clever as Mary was in the previous poem, but in a different way. She is not about to tell us where her hiding place is or how to get there. Instead, she retains the mystery of location while revealing enough details to draw the reader into the poem. Whereas Mary's poem is a text that is an invitation into a secret place in the world, Julia's poem is a text that is an invitation into a place as special—the poem itself.

And So On

Many of the poetry and fiction ideas for fourth and fifth graders that are presented in the next two chapters could be presented to third-grade writers with good results. I suggest that after trying out some of these writing ideas, you examine the following two chapters for further possibilities.

5

Fourth- and Fifth-Grade Poetry: The Universe, Outer and Inner

Kiddom

Fourth- and fifth-grade kids are pretty much everything—sensitive, articulate, thoughtful—and they possess a lighthearted spirit that incorporates a sense of proportion and humor. They take themselves seriously, but not too. They revel in the throes of kiddom, tasting every one of its succulent moments for all it's worth. On some levels, they know what's in store for them in the next year or two; they understand instinctively that they will shed their child ways and begin to grope slowly and then too quickly toward adulthood. It propels them, skinned knees and with elbows akimbo, into as many adventures as possible, making time itself stretch golden even if it can't, finally, last. Fourth- and fifth-grade kids live solidly in and among their own society; they don't need us, the hovering grown-ups, to make decisions, settle disputes, establish fashions, or plan parties. They can do it themselves quite nicely, thanks anyhow.

In spite of growing interest in gossip, awkward crushes, and sharply hurt feelings at one another's slights, fourth and fifth grade is also a time of deep, sometimes spiritual, reflection. By now, these kids have learned to use language, both spoken and written, with an ease that renders it second nature. They have learned to organize the manifold parts of the world in such a way that they can think about it abstractly, even philosophically. Fourth and fifth graders discover a passion for at least one aspect of the natural world during this time; great wheeling galaxies of stars, unsounded depths of oceans, fossils, caves, flora and fauna. Other cultures, whether shrouded in the ancient past or from the present yet geographically remote, are also compelling.

Embracing

My Heart Is

In the fall time
When red, yellow, orange leaves fall
I go to the woods and sit by the running creek.
I put a leaf in the sparkling water
I watch it glide down the fast flowing water
Then I hear the sound of deer
Scampering by me
I stop to look at squirrels gathering nuts.
This is where my heart is.

—*Emily F.*

Emily is anything but a quintessential fourth grader. On my first day with her class, she kept her tiny blond head bent and her shoulders hunched. She would not look at me during the group babble, when every other member of her class was enthusiastically tossing out contributions to the class discussion. Afterward, while the others scribbled pages and pages of stories, she sat with her pencil held so tightly that her knuckles turned white, and stared at her paper. She held her pencil tip not quite touching the paper and waited stoically for inspiration to hit. I had already been told that Emily didn't write on her own much and would curl up and die before she would read her work out loud to the class.

In spite of all this, something went click in her early on in the residency, and she discovered in herself not only a tactile love of language, but a ferocious need of it. In writing she discovered a means to say what is important in her life. At the end of the residency, we had a schoolwide poetry reading, to which parents and friends came. We held the reading in the school library, and we made a tape recording of it, which involved a lot of big, scary-looking equipment. Emily opened the reading, and read "My Heart Is" in a voice strong and sure of itself—her own new voice.

In this poem about passage, the author is less concerned with introducing herself than with establishing the temporal, natural frame in which the poem will unfold. Her first statement is about *when*—the "fall time." She focuses her lens more tightly in the second line, giving the abstract, conceptual "when" a physical, actual being—"when red, yellow, orange leaves fall." The repetition of "fall" turns the squat, inactive noun into a motion that spins the leaves, and the reader's eye, down deep into the woods, where the narrator is to be found, sitting by the running creek. The final image of squirrels gathering nuts effectively halts the endlessly spilling motion of the poem's activities. The leaves spill from the trees, the water flows quickly in the creek bed, a single leaf glides will-lessly along the surface of the water until it disappears from sight. Even the deer participates in this spilling forth, heard rather than seen, present only in its passage. The squirrels, however, reverse this rapid cascade by gathering in what will sustain them throughout the upcoming (implied) winter.

Emily's poem doesn't operate on such a complex and sophisticated level because she willed it so. This only points to the fact that to a large degree, strong poetry, kidmade or otherwise, doesn't consist of intellectually imposed technique and clever concept, but rises out of the body and out of experience. An intellectual appreciation of literature follows a primary sensual pleasure. Developmentally, we learn to read sometime after we learn to write. If we want our children to become astute readers, we must first encourage them to *embrace* (literally, "to clasp in the arms; hence, to cherish; love") the act of expressing who they are and what they think and feel through the written word.

Image and Lyrical Moments

Fourth- and fifth-grade writers, unlike those from first, second, and, to a lesser degree, third grades, understand the difference between writing that is essentially narrative and writing that is essentially lyrical. Narrative is strongly concerned with event—what occurs and what happens next as a natural outgrowth. Events have agents, and therefore narrative is also concerned with who is present and active—who causes the events to happen or whom the events happen to.

To very young writers, *who* and *me* are the same thing. They feel themselves strongly at the center not only of their own lives, but of life itself. By fourth grade, most students are pretty secure and comfortable with themselves in the world. The previous years of believing themselves to be the source of all experience has given them the courage to take steps forward into a new landscape where they are not at the center radiating outward, but merely one source of life among many. While they will still usually write in the first person—"I," when a narrator is present—they are willing to let go, becoming quiet and observant, as Emily was in the poem that opened this chapter. They are willing to consider the world as it is apart from them. At this point, they are ready to embrace experience lyrically.

Lyric, as opposed to narrative, is concerned not with event and activity but with emotion and atmosphere. A historical poem is narrative; a love poem is lyrical. While narrative writing is very much concerned with linking together a series of interinvolved moments, pushing itself forcefully through a stream of time to reach a conclusion, lyrical writing is concerned with freezing time's inevitable forward rush. If the narrative is a film, the lyric is a photograph, time frozen and framed for its simple, perfect beauty.

It is important to understand that while lyric poetry is about feelings and emotions, it is not about sentimentality. Sentimentality is the absence of vivid (literally "life-filled") emotion. It is the form of passionate feeling without the substance, the body without the beating heart. We adults like to pretend that childhood is all sweetness and soft edges. That's how we protect ourselves from our own fears for our children, and of them. It's disturbing when a child is passionate about something, because we fear she will lose control. What we really fear is that *we* have already lost control.

But life is not about being in control. It's about being passionately involved (involve, from Latin, means "to be within a roll"!), sometimes as an active participant, sometimes as a thoughtful and appreciative observer. Nobody knows this as well as a fourth grader, unless it's a fifth grader. When these kids write poetry that is lyrical in nature, they are concerned with the subtle, delicate shades of feeling they experience. They are tender with their words, for they know that in truth, feeling can't quite be captured by language. Like a soap bubble, it is fragile, and while it can be herded carefully through the air with gentle breaths, it cannot be touched directly or it will simply vanish.

The Worlds of Nature

The natural world, for fourth and fifth graders, offers a myriad of expressions of themselves.

The Effect of the Wind

The effect of the wind is
leaves swirling around
in eddies
green trees tilting to one side
paper whirling around the
street
and your house
quivering and shaking
at every moment.

—Tim K.

Night

When night leaves it goes home.
It sings different songs every night.
It sings by tapping the branches of trees on windows.
Night dreams about making music . . . (excerpt)

—Evelyn R.

The Wind

The wind is a gentle breeze
That sways back and forth
Over the daffodils & Maple Trees.
But sometimes it whizzes over
You like a howling monster
And makes the Maple Trees
spread out and the daffodils
bend over.

—Stephanie M.

Wind

. . . You
blow the petals of the flowers gentle
You swift a way with the leaves . . . (excerpt)

—Kerian McD.

The Wind

The wind is like a whole symphony orchestra.
You hear birds sing in the wind
They sing like flutes in the wind

> Sometimes the wind will get mad,
> It sounds like the beating of drums.
> It can get very mean and sound like
> a whole concert,
> singing rocking roll .... (excerpt)
>
> —*Mark C.*

Night

> The night's moon shone through
> the finger shaped tree top.
> The stars sparkled brightly
> in the howling wind,
> while I drifted into another world
> to the sound of a owl's hoot.
>
> —*Tracy S.*

The previous six poems are really about only two things—the night and the wind. Yet no two are alike in language, image, or concept. Each of the poets wrote out of his or her own deeply felt vision.

Poetry and Inspiration

Fourth or fifth grade is not too early to introduce the students to the poetry of respected contemporary writers. A word of advice: keep it simple. If you aren't familiar with the abundance of contemporary American and world poets, educate yourself first. Pick up a few anthologies. Buy some literary magazines, or check them out of the library. Bring in mimeo or Xerox copies for each child. These copies should be kept in their writing folders, along with their own work. Read the poem out loud while they listen with closed eyes. Have them read silently to themselves. Have them read out loud alone at home. Treat the poem like a sacred teaching. Puzzle over mysterious lines together: what does it mean; what could it mean? But don't limit yourself to trying to discover meaning; ask as well what the poem makes the reader feel. Don't accept "good." What is good?—content, sad, peaceful, angry, enthusiastic? Really listen to their answers. Break these discussions into smaller groups. This will prepare them for critiquing one another's work later on. This is important: any one of your students is allowed to hate any one of the poems you bring in. But whether they like a poem or find it revolting, they *do* have to be able to tell you what it is that affects them.

This past year I have presented James Dickey's poem "The Heaven of

Animals" to several different classes. I was surprised, frankly, to find that my fifth-grade classes were as able to find pleasure and meaning in the poem as my high school classes:

The Heaven of Animals

Here they are. The soft eyes open.
If they have lived in a wood
It is a wood.
If they have lived on plains
It is grass rolling
Under their feet forever.

Having no souls, they have come,
Anyway, beyond their knowing.
Their instincts wholly bloom
And they rise.
The soft eyes open.

To match them, the landscape flowers,
Outdoing, desperately
Outdoing what is required:
The richest wood,
The deepest field.

For some of these,
It could not be the place
It is, without blood.
These hunt, as they have done,
But with claws and teeth grown perfect,

More deadly than they can believe.
They stalk more silently,
And crouch on the limbs of trees,
And their descent
Upon the bright backs of their prey

May take years
In a sovereign floating of joy.
And those that are hunted
Know this as their life,
Their reward: to walk

Under such trees in full knowledge
Of what is in glory above them,
And to feel no fear,
But acceptance, compliance.
Fulfilling themselves without pain

At the cycle's center,
They tremble, they walk
Under the tree,
They fall, they are torn,
They rise, they walk again.

—James Dickey

After talking at length about the poem, the kids closed their eyes and visualized different kinds of heavens, while I asked prompt questions quietly in the background. Many of the heavens had to do with specific animals, thus doubly linking them with the Dickey poem. But they wrote as well on the heavens of pencil stubs, evening gowns, geodes, rocking chairs, mirrors and bicycle pumps!

The Deer's Heaven

The heaven of deers is
Green grassy fields with
pink tulips and roses with
All different kinds of trees
When it rains the water is
Like crystal drops falling
Down. The deers gracefully
Run through the everlasting
Fields. The wind in this heaven is
Spring breezes that flow.
The deer's heaven is where
Only the deers know.

—Stephanie M.

Notice Thomas C's subtle use of snakelike sibilance in the following poem.

The Heaven of Snakes

In the heaven of snakes,
You can see and hear the long snakes
Slithering through the long, green grass
Searching for food.
Slithering and sliding
With their beautiful, silky skin,
Hissing softly,
Wrapping around branches . . . (excerpt)

—Thomas C.

The Sports Heaven

The land upstairs is the perfect land
The Yankees and Mets never lose
Babe Ruth gets a homerun everytime
up
If you strike out . . .
Don't worry it's
The land of perfect

—*Leo O.*

The Animal World

Kids love animals, and so do poets. Pick up poetry anthologies at the library or bookstore and search out a few poems about animals you think your kids will like. I use Robert Bly's "The Turtle" and Theodore Roethke's "The Heron." During the group premeditation discussion, encourage the writers to come up with a list of all kinds of wild and domestic beasts. Ask for details—where they can commonly be found, what they eat, what family units are like. I suggest banishing pets as subject matter. Kids get all tangled up in how cute their pets are, and are often unable to get beyond that. Also, make a comprehensive list on the board of words that are imageless but in danger of popping up (*cute, adorable, funny, brave,* etc.) During the meditation, repeatedly ask the writers to visualize a single animal in a very specific place. Remind them they are like scientists, studying their visions for subtle, easily overlooked details. Ask for sounds, smells, colors, textures, tiny details, weather, light, imperfections that will make the image strong.

Swan

. . . The swan swims in a blackened
misty lake trees and flowers
of blue, red, purple, and pink
surrounding it. The swan
swims like a kite
gliding in the air. When the
swan gets out of the water
it waddles around like a
pendulum in a clock swaying
back and forth. Its feet
are a light orange with

a tint of yellow and it
has webbed toes. They look
like the edge of a spider web
sitting in the breeze . . . . (excerpt)

—*Jennifer M.*

The Salamander

The salamander slips
under a rock
With the rushing
water.
And the dim light.
The blue sky.
It climbs a tree very fast.
Hides under a rock or
blends in with another tree
Then crawls away
and is gone for now
or maybe forever.
But then it comes back
unexpectedly, and quickly.

—*Daniel R.*

The Emotional World

The flower of loneliness
lies in the trampled land
of the Middle East.
Where a
war is being fought.
Where the people
are being killed.
No sun, just dark gray clouds
fill the air.
The flower of loneliness description
is hardly known.
But we know it's there.
The flower stands 1 foot tall.
It is the color musty gray
with a black
stem.

> One or two
> can be found on the
> dirty and sandy battlefield.
>
> —*Yann*

This poem is anything but sentimental; the bleak landscape, the sunless sky, the sparse black-and-gray flowers, metaphors, we feel, for the newly dead, combine to both express Yann's concern and to pull us, the readers, from our daily lives for a moment, really to think about our world and what we do to one another. This poem is effective because of its images, its attention to detail, and its own feelings. Yann doesn't tell us in the poem that his brother is stationed in the Middle East; but nonetheless, we can feel what he feels, the sorrow and bewilderment.

Metaphor

The definition of metaphor I memorized in ninth grade was, "Metaphor is the direct comparison of two unlike objects without using the words *like* or *as*". Functional, but entirely too pat. In truth, metaphor is a terrifically elusive concept. Think about it: how can two things that are totally different be spoken of as if they were the same? The answer is, because of the creative abilities of the human mind to synthesize. Metaphor is an identification of two things that are in fact physically distinct. It establishes a resonance between two objects that are in fact separate and unrelated.

Simile is basically realistic metaphor—comparing two unlike things using *like* or *as*. Simile finds similarities. "The sun unfurls its petals" is a metaphor, because it finds the similarities between the sun and a flower so strong that the two are fused (temporarily at least) into a single identity. "The sun is like a flower unfurling its petals" is a simile; it does not lose its head and insist upon total identification between two such obviously distinct things. It is more culturally realistic.

In order to think about a thing when it isn't there, we need a mental image. Words are the names for mental images. Language itself permits us to think about the world by organizing and categorizing the plethora of sense stimuli that would otherwise overwhelm us. Metaphor finds identification between things that are, in reality, distinct. But in reality all things are distinct, all things are unique, isolated instances of their own being. Our minds are clever little things. On the one hand, they are complex and creative enough to allow us to invent language, by which we communicate, by which we develop incredibly sophisticated societies in which we forget we are, after all, animals. On the other hand, our minds are limited, for we absolutely cannot speak of every isolated object and event the world has ever known, and if we tried, we would indeed have a Tower of Babel where nothing, in the end, is namable or communicable. Each tree is different, but each tree shares a common spirit, a "tree-ness." The legs on a human are absolutely not the same thing as table legs, or the last leg of a race, or not having a leg to stand on. But they do all share the idea of support.

At the heart of our human ability to make language is metaphor. At the core of our human ability to bridge the gaps between our isolated selves is poetry.

Get the Essence

Last year I began exploring the idea of metaphor with Mrs. Bennett's fourth grade at Sargent School in Beacon, New York. We began class with a meditation. The room was darkened, and the kids all had their heads down. Their breathing was deep and slow, their eyes closed, their faces, open.

"Everything in the world is really like something else. One thing can look or feel like another or have the same shape. Maybe the sameness is on the inside—two things with the same spirit. You really have to be slow and sensitive to catch the sameness between two things that are different; you really have to feel it with your guts as well as with your heads."

They breathed in unison, and sighed, and sunk deeper into the meditation.

"Sometimes somebody makes a comparison that everybody else starts using. Pretty soon, it gets used so much we forget the picture that goes with it. He's as big as a barn, she's as thin as a stick, are comparisons that have lost their zing, because we've heard them before. We call them clichés. A strong metaphor compares two things in a new way, two things that haven't been compared before.

"Really imagine the sun now, in your mind. Look at its color, look at its light. Is there anything in the sky near it? What color, exactly is the sky? Where is the sun you see in your mind, in relation to the horizon? What does the sun remind you of? What other thing is the sun like? What has the same spirit as the sun?"

After the lights were switched back on, and they raised their heads, blinking sleepily in the fluorescent glare, I asked them again.

"What is the sun like? What does it remind you of?"

The first few answers were qualities of the sun and memories concerning the sun; not unexpected, as the idea of metaphor is something of a stretch for fourth graders close to the beginning of the school year.

"Hot."

"Like fire."

"Round."

"Yellow."

"Okay," I told them, "those are all things that are true about the sun. It's yellow, at least part of the time, it's made out of fire, and therefore it's hot. It's round, all right. What else is just that kind of round?"

"A ball."

"A cookie."

"Dig deeper," I pushed. "Close your eyes and see it again."

"Uhnnn!" screamed somebody in the back row, attached to a wildly waving arm. "When I was in Florida I saw orange trees and oranges were growing on branches and this one orange was growing way out on a branch and it looked like it was floating in the sky like the sun at sunrise!" He smiled.

I smiled. The whole class grinned. "Yup," I said. "You got it. Somebody give me another one. What else shares its spirit?"

"A dandelion, because of the yellow."

"A lion, because its hotness is like a lion's . . . everything, and the lion has a ruffle of fur like the sun has rays."

Not bad, not great.

I called on a kid with rasta dredlocks and a bright rainbow-striped beret.

"The sun is like walking around in grass thinking about flowers." He tilted his head back and fixed me with a look of satisfaction. "That's what it *is*. That's its essence."

I almost fell over backward. How could a nine-year-old know the word *essence* and know that that is exactly what a metaphor does? Metaphor identifies the essence of one thing, and finds something apparently different with the same essence. Look up *essence* in the dictionary, and you find it comes from the Latin root, *esse*; "to be"! By definition, *essence* means a thing's basic nature, its being.

Before I had a chance to respond, he was interrupted.

"Say that again, man," his best friend ordered.

"I said the sun was like walking around in the grass thinking about flowers."

I sighed with pure pleasure. And to think I once considered becoming an accountant.

"Write it on the board, poet," the best friend said to me. I wrote it dutifully down.

"You said it wrong," the best friend stated firmly. "You didn't think the verbs out and you didn't say the specificist nouns." He crossed his arms on his chest and nodded once, to indicate his agreement with himself.

A shy redheaded boy with freckles murmured, "roaming."

Then a girl in a miniature mechanic's jumpsuit: "strolling."

The alternatives to *walking* began to come fast and furiously. I scrawled a rapid list on the blackboard, and didn't stop until the chalk snapped. I wrote:

roam	hop
stroll	wander
amble	storm
drift	stomp
trot	trudge
limp	glide
hobble	drag

"Which ones do you like best? Each type of walking is a little different," I said.

"Not storm or stomp," somebody tossed out.

"Not hop or hobble or limp or trot. Too quick."

"Yeah. We don't want anything too quick. We want something nice and slow and cool."

"Cool?" I asked. "But the sun is hot."

"Cool. Laid back, easy. Like how it makes you feel all lazy in the summertime. Amble or wander," came the answer.

I crossed out *walking* and wrote beneath it *ambling* and *wandering*. Next we looked at *in the grass*. The class consensus was that it was too vague. They tried *on a hillside*, but somebody said it made her feel like she was going to fall off. Someone threw out field, and that led straight to meadow. Everybody liked that. The board now read:

> The sun is like walking (ambling, wandering) around in the grass (meadow) thinking about flowers.

Thinking was the next word under examination, and they had a lot of trouble with it. They came up with *considering, looking at, studying, examining, meditating, visualizing*. Finally, somebody suggested dreaming, because that's thinking when you're asleep. *Flowers* was easy; they had to be yellow because the sun is yellow. A few kids wanted to name specific yellow flowers—daffodils, dandelions, tulips—but everyone else liked *yellow flowers* because it implied all kinds of yellow flowers without having to list them. We now had:

> The sun is like walking (ambling, wandering) around in the grass (meadow) thinking (dreaming) about yellow flowers.

A tall girl with glasses shot up her hand. "I don't like the way 'around in' sounds. Can't we say 'through the meadow' instead?"

"Sure," I said, and made the change on the board.

"We wrote 'yellow' before for the flowers; we should write 'green' now for the meadow. To make it match. And we should say 'green meadows' instead of 'the green meadow.'" The speaker held out two hands like she was weighing something, balanced them for a second, and shrugged:

> The sun is like walking (ambling, wandering) through green meadows dreaming about yellow flowers.

"I like wandering," a big sleepy kid (who sat directly in front of me because he liked to make trouble), said abruptly. "I don't know why; I just do."

I crossed out *ambling*.

> The sun is like wandering through green meadows dreaming about yellow flowers.

I figured we were done, but the boy with rasta hair wanted the last word. "'Of,'" he said. "Not 'about'; 'of.'" Okay, 'of.' I wrote it:

> The sun is like wandering through green meadows dreaming of yellow flowers.

The class was so taken with the energy of group effort that we did another simile. It started out as:

> Snow is like climbing up a big white mountain and feeling the air get more cold and hearing the birds louder.

The class went to work on it. Several steps later it became:

> Snow is like climbing up a quiet white mountain and feeling the soft breeze sweep your face and hearing the sweet singing of birds.

Incidentally, the kids were fully aware of the sounds they were working with. After we were done, the whole group erupted into what I can only describe as the sweet sound of singing birds. Nearly every child read the words softly out loud, not in chorus, but individually, tasting the sounds.

"Hey," somebody said suddenly, "breeze, sweep, sweet'! The 'eeze, eep, eet' kinda rhyme! And 'sw, sw.' Hey, we're good!"

I had expected the standard metaphor/simile stuff from these kids—a comparison of one object to another. Until Mrs. Bennett's fourth-grade class, it never occurred to me that kids could make the jump to comparing an object to an event; finding an essential identity between a noun and a verb.

A few months and considerable thought later, I decided to try the same idea with another fourth grade—Mrs. Pierson's class in Perry, New York. This time, though, instead of seeking a metaphor for an object, we looked for a metaphor for an emotional state. We began by making a list of emotional states on the board:

anger	enthusiasm
joy	greed
shyness	arrogance
amazement	silliness
jealousy	horror
sorrow	timidity
loneliness	irritation
generosity	affection

I made an arbitrary decision and selected *shyness*. The class was small, and as a group a little shy. I wondered what they would come up with. We made another list of places on the board:

waterfall	beach
volcano	mountaintop
cornfield	creek
valley	woods
cave	canyon

Certain places, they agreed, seemed more shy than others. A valley, a creek, and the woods were the three places they chose. I arbitrarily selected woods. During the meditation, I asked them to visualize the place of shyness, the woods where shyness dwells. I asked for who or what they saw, sounds they heard, weather conditions. Here is the first group draft:

Shyness

Rabbits scamper in the quiet woods.
Light snow falls onto the trees.
The lake stands all alone.

We talked about how small shyness feels, how small and yet full of pictures the poem was. Someone suggested we cross out all the *the*'s because we didn't need them. Other changes were offered, argued over, accepted, or rejected. Here is the poem in its final version:

Shyness

Rabbits scamper in quiet woods
Light snow drifts to empty frosted meadow
Frozen lake reflects pine tree

I looked at the poem and looked at the class. "This is like a haiku," I started to tell them, but of course they already knew. Their teacher showed me some haiku they had written earlier in the school year—I could see by their poems that not only were they sensitive to the profundity of the quiet, small moments in life, but that obviously so was their teacher. If I haven't made it clear yet, this is a perfect moment to stress what a difference there is in children's writing when their teacher has led them toward a love of language and a means of self-expression.

Evolving

You, as a teacher, know it is important to let your teaching continuously evolve. You don't, I'm sure, approach the same lessons in the same exact way you did a few years ago. Teaching is one of the most demanding professions there is, and burnout happens to everybody. Part of the trick is to keep your spirit enthused at the same time you are endlessly putting out energy and love and attention. You can't keep yourself enthused if you get stuck, paralyzed, and fossilized in endless repetition. You have to be able to respond to the people who are your students. That means changing your assignments, how you approach them, how you teach them. A lesson begins with an insight and evolves. The metaphor lesson that began in Beacon evolved in Perry and turned into something entirely different. By the time I reached North Babylon, Long Island, the lesson had completely transformed.

The class began as usual, by making a comprehensive verbal list of feelings, and discussing metaphor. After that, we made three lists on the board:

Landscapes

cave	zoo
meadow	swamp
arbor	desert
beach	city

Objects

scissors	silver dollar
glue	sink
earrings	feather
telephone	letter

Dwellings

hut	barn
castle	lean-to
treehouse	condo
shed	split-level

The meditation simply asks what landscape, object, and dwelling has the same spirit as a particular feeling.

Sorrow

Sorrow is a clock
It ticks and ticks
it is an orphanage
filled with sadness.
Sorrow is a scissor
it cuts you up inside
your heart.
Sorrow is a mirror
it looks right back at you.
Sorrow is a cave a
lonely hollow place.
Sorrow is a lock
it locks you up inside yourself.

—*Jeanne G.*

Shyness

Shyness is a mist
on a early
spring morning in a
forest near a
sprinkling waterfall,
as the sun rises
a little morning dove
flies over and perches
itself on a
mighty fir tree

—Laura B.

Fear

Fear is like a Earth Quake waiting to
crack open
When it cracks things we worked
hard for are gone
That's what fear is
Fear is like a swamp
Knowing its not going to move
Fear is fear in its own way
We all know fear so please
stay away.

—Richard D.

This last poem's effectiveness is not only due to the identification between fear, the earthquake, and the unmoving swamp, but because, having made those comparisons, it refuses them. "Fear is fear in its own way," the poem states simply, having tried comparisons and found them wanting. This stripping the poem of its devices leaves the last two lines "We all know fear so please/stay away" laid starkly bare. I would like to include two more poems in this section on metaphor. They were both the products of the same class at Parliament Place in North Babylon. I read the students some kids' poems that exemplified metaphor, and we talked about the images they placed in our heads. This time, however, I didn't lead the class in a detailed visualization of a single, pre-established image. Instead, I asked the writers to grab hold of one of the many images that were floating around in their heads at that moment. They homed in tighter and tighter on the image in their minds, each writer picturing something unique, something that came out of the marriage of experience and imagination. As they watched, the image slowly by slowly turned into something else—the perfect metaphor, naturally arrived at.

A Romantic Sight

The moon round as a crystal ball,
glistens in the long dark blanket—
of night.
Its reflection shows
its vast face
amongst the sleeping
flamingos

—Melissa M.

At first I was baffled by Melissa's poem; it didn't seem as though it could have come from a fifth grader: it's too graceful, too elegant. She wrote it in class, but I wondered if it had somehow superimposed itself into her mind from a book or card. After I got to know her, I discovered all her work has this voice, this flavor. She is a writer, and she knows it. She reads poetry as well as writing it; note (its hard not to) her use of the poetic *among'st*. When I asked if she knew where her idea came from, she told me about a painting that her mother had. The images of the moon and the sleeping flamingos had so impressed themselves upon her that the poem emerged, all in a rush, when it was triggered by her meditation.

I am fortunate enough to have a yellow piece of paper covered with three drafts of a metaphor poem by a student named Peter. I really treasure this collection, not just for the marvelous final version, but for the glimpse into the mind of the young writer it affords. I will do my best to reproduce it here:

the sleek moving wolf xxxxxxx[illegible] pounced
hunch backed upon the unexpected
deer like a frogs tounge
wihping onto the wings
of a parilized frog.

The sleek moving wolf
ponced upon the fragile

The sleek moving
wolf
pounced upon the fragile unexpecting
deer

> like a frog's tongue whipping onto
> a helpless fly's wings.
>
> —*Peter M.*

In the first two versions it is easy to see Peter working out not only the images he wanted, but the syntax. He canned *hunch backed* immediately in the first draft, because it clearly wasn't a consistent image. *Unexpected* is the wrong adjective to describe the deer, but we know what he meant, and so did he, because it was easily corrected by the final draft. His repetition of *frog* was likewise an error, not of judgment or vision, but of habit. His mind was racing, his hand was racing to keep up with it, and he didn't stop to edit or worry himself about the process at all. In the first draft he worked out a record of his basic idea. This is not much different from the drawings a first grader will use for inspiration. Notice, too, that Peter's spelling in the first draft is pretty wildly out of control. He doesn't seem concerned with that either, and he shouldn't be, because in a first draft, it matters not a whit.

A lot of the working out clearly occurred in his mind only, for by the third draft not only has his spelling improved, but his line breaks contribute to the overall effect of the poem. In setting *wolf* and *deer* apart from the rest of the poem, he clarifies the relationships involved: wolf is to deer as frog's tongue is to fly's wings. I find it particularly marvelous that the essential equivalencies are not merely highly unusual animals (a wolf and a frog? a deer and a fly?) but those portions of their bodies that simultaneously characterize them and that are necessary to their survival—a frog's tongue and a fly's wings!

From the Beginning to the End and Back Again

While reading Claudia Lewis's marvelous book *A Big Bite of the World,* I came across the following poem, written by a sixth-grade boy:

A Death Song

> Could this be it!
> A soft humming
> as I sunk to the ground,
> the birds chattering, the leaves
> falling, they all seemed
> to fade away through
> darkness and then I knew
> that I must go slowly

slowly. I must go.
Good-bye, good-bye, good-bye life.

I was caught not only by the images of the chattering birds amid the falling leaves and then the rising darkness, but by the simplicity and integrity with which this young writer considers his own death. He does not approach it sentimentally; there are no regrets and no tears here. Nor is he concerned with grounding it in a narrative context/situation. Indeed, the poem is about how dying feels and is—matters of the spirit—not about the worldly details leading up to the event. I read the poem aloud to the group just before class ended. They were quiet after I read, and then one asked me to read it again.

"It isn't sad at all—dying," someone commented.

Silence.

"I wonder about it sometimes," another voice remarked. Several kids nodded in agreement. I told them that I did, too. As we talked, we realized that a lot of us pictured it the way the poem described it, slow and soft and darkening, perhaps sweetly regretful, but peaceful nontheless.

The kids came into class the following day in much the same mood. We talked for a while longer about the last moments a person has on earth, the feelings and thoughts and sensations that might rise out of a lifetime of experiences to stand strong in the final moments. After a while, without my directing it, the conversation turned to birth. We talked about the first things a baby sees (lights, the doctor in a face mask, the table, the crib, a stuffed bear) and hears (its own voice crying, people talking, car doors, the music coming from the wind-up mobile of stars and a moon that hangs over the crib). We talked about the fact that because the baby has never seen or heard these things before, it doesn't have any idea what they are.

At some point in the conversation, I reminded the students about the work with metaphor they had done in the previous two days. During the meditation, they were urged to return to the moments of their birth and first day, to remember its sensations and nothing else. Then, I asked them to visualize a metaphor, an essential equivalent, for the experience they were feeling. The resulting poems were sweet, full of fantasy and yet reflective of reality:

Birth

I was sitting on a stump in
my back yard
eating strawberries and listening

to my record player.
I saw a butterfly go by I ran after
it.
I saw a bee picking on my
strawberries.
It saw me coming and I
thought it flew away
but it didn't.
It was behind me
Next thing I knew it stung me.

—*Kristen P.*

I wonder; is the bee's sting a metaphor for the doctor's slapping hand?

Birth

Waiting in a park,
I opened my
eyes
discovering the baby blue
sky,
Watching the clouds turn
into sheep that
jump and dance over the
sun

—*Monica H.*

Birth

As I step out of a dark hole
I see things I've never seen before
A bright yellow ball in a blue
layer of cloth
I see crystal clear liquid running in a muddy
ditch.
These things so
new and
so beautiful

—*Jacquie Marie W.*

I like the fact that this last poem opens in the middle of an action, "As I step out"—implying that birth is not the beginning and the source of life, but one of the resting points along a circular journey.

The poems on birth offer the sweetness of childhood remembered—meadows and singing insects, bright yellows and blues and greens, the colors of a child's nursery, a park, clouds that turn into leaping sheep, dancing across the sun—everything bright with its own newness. Of course a baby would believe that the first time she beheld a tree or a cloud or cricket was the moment in which it first came into being, and therefore, was new!

Birth II

when I finally stopped running
and caught my breath
I was in the middle of
a green carpet
in front of me were
red roses
I picked one
but was pricked
I turned my head in pain (excerpt)

—*Katie S.*

Birth

As I looked around
I saw lots of straw and hay
I got up on a horse and pranced
I milked the cows and helped my
friend make butter
we collected eggs from the
chickens and hens
the mistress said we could clip
wool from the sheep

—*Michelle L.*

Michelle was particularly thoughtful after writing this poem. She came up to the desk while the others were still working and asked if she could read it out loud to the class. After she read it, one of the other writers pointed out that it sounded like a place from the past; another student had the words for it—"medieval times." Michelle nodded slowly, "The picture I got was like I was there before," she said. Needless to say, it isn't possible to have this kind of conversation go on among twenty-six fifth graders without at least three of them bringing up the subject of reincarnation. I let them talk and I listened. That led to yet another transformation of the metaphor assignment, which I will go into in depth a little farther on in this chapter.

Contemplating the first moments of life as a philosophical/spiritual question appealed to most of the fourth and fifth graders who encountered it as a subject for poetry. But the students at Beacon, and later, other young writers, also wanted to write about death. At first I resisted. I think it is of utmost importance to be cautious about teaching creative writing assignments by the book from the book (including this one) for the simple reason that unless you are personally charged by and involved with the ideas behind the assignment, they ultimately will not contain the spark of life and energy that is essential to creation. I seem always to end up using other people's writing assignments only for inspiration to transform them into something else. After some thought, I decided it's fine to borrow other teachers' assignments:

1. We are all connected to one another through infinite inescapable nets of language, culture, economics, art, food, and almost anything else you can name. History and culture tie us together. Nobody, or almost nobody, lives alone at the top of a mountain anymore. (Oh, I know there are a few who keep trying, but look what happens. They get a constant stream of devotees traipsing up and down looking for enlightenment and wrecking the privacy and the view, not to mention smashing the foliage.) Given the fact that we are all so interrelated, it's fine sometimes to borrow a writing topic or style of approach almost verbatim.

2. Who am I to say a bunch of curious fifth-grade writers can't write about death?

3. I rail with perfect righteousness against butterfly, rainbow, puppydog and unicorn poems, pointing to their lack of depth, to the fact they are written only to please sentimental adults. But when the kids asked to write poems about death, a truly deep subject, I got nervous. I became afraid that I wouldn't be able to guide them through the subject matter without one or two falling off into angst or fear or the rekindled pain of the death of someone they knew. But they were asking to write about something real, disturbing to them *because* it is not allowed as material for consideration in their daily

lives. Adults don't like to admit the fact of death into the lives of their children. And I too had fallen into that cultural expectation: kids shouldn't think about, talk about, or worry about death. But they do, and not all of their concern is anxiety laden. Some of it is healthy curiosity, interest that really isn't morbid or perverse at all.

Death

The last thing I saw before
I died was my house.
Then I went to this place
It was full of colors.
There were lots of people there.
It was bright.
Some of my old friends were
there.
It felt like I was home.
It smelt like flowers.
You can taste the air.

—Michelle M.

Death

I'm still an old man still
walking around in my house.
Grey hair grey beard too.
All the sudden I saw pitch black.
That's all I see for hours, and
hours.

—Chris P.

I like the way the element of time plays in the above poem. "I'm still an old man," written by a nine-year-old, is fascinating, for he is writing about his distant future at one remove; he's been an old man in the poem for a long time. There is also the interesting hinge of " still/walking around in my house"—wherein *still* suggests silence and motionlessness, but means, when it intersects with the next line, "continuing." Death comes as a pitch black vision, but that's not the end: it's simply what the narrator sees for hours, implying that beyond the pitch black lies other things about which he cannot or will not speak.

Death

I am in my bed in the hospital
and I fall asleep in my dream
I was walking in a dark foggy forest
and my grandfather was calling
me and I heard his voice and I took one
step back and fell off the cliff but
I never hit the ground

—Anthony B.

The Second Time Around

When we were kids, my cousin Carol once told me I was brave because I wasn't afraid to wear bizarre clothes and do my hair in weird, self-inflicted styles and say strange things. Her compliment crushed me. I remember myself as a child who tried hard to be like everyone else! I will admit I just want to be liked, and to that end, will do almost anything. I've tried carefully to clip the edges of my natural-born weirdness and fold them under, grooming myself into something resembling social acceptability. I'm careful not to rock too many boats. In spite of all this tailoring, I'm nervous about being unacceptable. So I avoid certain things, like encouraging the kids to write about "forbidden" topics, such as death and previous lives.

But this year, something clicked inside me, and I started listening to the kids talk among themselves. They are serious philosophers, spiritually attuned, anthropologically curious, and unafraid to examine all kinds of inexplicable things like mental telepathy, magical powers and abilities, and life after death. The idea of reincarnation is a great way to teach the idea of metaphor. Kids are tickled by the idea that they may have previously been a place, an event, a weather condition, a small object that can be held in the hand, or a state of mind or emotion. Some of them choose to write with a great deal of tongue-in-cheek humor (like the boy who turned in a poem titled "My Past Tense"), while others are inspired to delve more deeply than ever before into the question of who they are and where they came from.

Birthstone

I am a pebble tumbling and mumbling to myself.
I dream I'm with other stones.

I dream I'm in a desert in a cave sitting with myself.
I love being a pebble because when I want to be alone I can be
alone.
I do lots of crazy things like when I go outside sliding and
riding, tumbling just to see dusk.
I don't know why I put myself in all that commotion.
But being a stone is a lot of motion.

—*L'Amour S.*

This poem is quintessentially L'Amour's spirit: she is a solid, absolutely silent girl, slow moving, deliberate, observant. Yet she reveals that the life of a stone, her own metaphor for herself, is filled with activity—sliding, tumbling, mumbling, riding—just for the satisfaction of beholding the beauty of dusk.

I. Me

In my pre-birth, I was
a tiny white pebble, being kicked
off a tall boulder on a mountain
side. As I fell, I tumbled through
what seemed like infinity, rolling
and flipping, until finally I landed
with a soft thud on the young spring
grasses, their heads shooting up through
the warm, brown earth with such pride
I hated to bend their shoots. There I
nestled for many years. I was buried
and faded, rubbed and scraped until I
was nothing but a small grain of sand.
And then I was nothing.

II. Myself

Before my conception, I was
a small, perfectly oval, crystal
blue spring. I gurgled forth
virgin water every now and then.
Around me there were crystalized
pebbles scattered over the pale green
grass. Their bodies twinkled and flashed
when the dappled sunlight
came shooting down from the
cobweb of leaves and landed
on them.

I was a well kept
secret, for the only knowledgeable
living thing of me were the
trees in the forest. I was never
drank from, ever, in my short existence
as the clear blue spring.

III. And, I

You've never seen me before,
for I fly high in the treetops.
Some have seen my gorgeous flash
of pale yellow, bright turquoise, and
burning magenta. I am
the Bird of Paradise, who is a mystery
to all mankind.

—*Rebecca H.*

There is a wonderful circularity, a relatedness of parts in the above poem. Rebecca poetically begins life as a pebble tumbling through infinity, which is finally worn down to nothing. Then she returns as a spring, which is surrounded by pebbles much like herself in the previous lifetime. She is protected by the forest's trees. Finally, she transforms into a bird that reveals itself only through a flash of color high in what we feel to be the same trees!

Portraits

What is a portrait, whether of yourself or of someone else? A likeness—but what makes one portrait good and another boring? Throw this question open to a classroom of kids. Bring in some snapshots, photos cut from magazines, or of famous paintings, and prepare to be entertained. A really good portrait is a good likeness, which, as any kid will be glad to tell you, isn't taken when Mom has just had her hair done and is wearing her best dress and inherited pearls, but when the toast is burning, the dog has just thrown up on the carpet, and the phone is ringing off the hook. If a portrait is going to *portray* (from Latin, "to draw forth") the subject truly, it must capture that subject in a characteristic place in the midst of familiar activity. A good portrait is about someone other than the author (unless, of course, it is a self-portrait). Therefore, the portrait is largely about what the author sees the subject doing, not about what the author feels about the subject's actions. The portrait is about one person in one place doing something; it is framed by time and by space. Your kids might be desperate to write portraits about people they know well (older cousins with hot cars, warm Italian grammas with cookie-scented kitchens) or about people they don't know but have seen (a bum sleeping under a park bench, or the guy who runs the dog pound). Stress the careful noting and selecting of details, and stress, as usual, as always, smells and sounds, textures, colors, tastes. Here are some portraits to read to your kids to get them tuned in and running:

The Waiter

The person, the person I see
of course,
Is the waiter on the train.
When the train sways back
and forth,
Not a piece of food does he drop,
not even a piece as small as a pea.
Oh the waiter with the
red apron and white jacket,
If you're sitting alone he'll
give you some company,
he'll lead you to your comfortable seat
Where you'll sit and eat on
the train, the train that you
can hear the clattering and
banging of the wheels,
while the train goes through the bay.

—*Janelle K.*

With her occasional repetitions ("the person/the person I see; the train/the train that you" . . .), Janelle suggests the rhythmic, hypnotic sound of the train rolling along the track.

My Grandfather Is

My Grandfather is lazy
he sits in his chair
he leaves the alarm
clock on and the TV too
his hair is a mess he
leaves the dying flowers
on the floor the dead

ones in the vase and
the scissors on the floor
he leaves the bird in its
messy cage.

—*Kristi Z.*

The Big Wrestler

Hulk is in a big square wrestling
ring. He hears the bell ringing loudly.
He feels the rough skin of his opponent
as he whips him into the ropes.
He sees the fans waving their
American flags. He tastes the
wet sweat as it trickles into his
mouth. He stretches his muscular
python arms as he slams his
opponent to the mat. He feels the
struggling of the man as he pins him.

—*Mike S.*

Mike is wrestling himself here, with line breaks. The poem reflects Hulk's situation. All action takes place in the square ring (notice the boxlike shape of the poem). The readers' attention is splintered repeatedly from one thing to another, and this is mimicked by the fractured phrases whose lines are broken against their own logical division. There is an intense focus and insistence upon the experience of the moment.

Portrait of My Ice Cream Man

When I get some ice cream
from the ice cream man
I watch him very closely.
He scoops gobs of ice cream
on a cone and smiles
I pay him and the
next customer comes.
He wears a checkered apron
and a white coned hat.
When he laughs his belly
sinks in and out like the ocean waves.
His beard looks like
a thorn bush.

—*Joel A.*

What is remarkable about this poem is not only the very careful, quiet attention to detail, but the fact that he creates a sense of place only through his similes. The ice cream man's belly becomes the ocean waves, while his beard is a thorn bush.

When My Cousin Nicky Builds with His Legos

When he builds his fortress out of legos he sticks his
tongue out on the side of his mouth.
His eyebrows shrivel up and he sits on his knees. When he
is done with his masterpiece he collapses onto the couch to watch
TV

—Gregory V.

Clearly, the author's attention in this poem is to images—or is it? Like the Hulk poem, the line breaks seem illogical and haphazard, part of a phrase stuck onto another, a statement broken unnaturally part way through. It seems that the author didn't plan the line breaks through ahead of time. Why, he wrote the poem as if he were building something out of legos!

My Teacher

When my teacher
in a green suit
started to write
a great
poem
She suddenly
looked to see
if everyone
was nice
and quiet
Then she wiggled
a little

—Toni W.

When the Eye Looks at the I

The poems that result from a meditation on one's own self are often both deeply peaceful and subtle. Suggest, during the meditation, that each writer visualize herself at a particular time of year, in a particular weather, in a very special, specific place. It isn't necessary that the writer has been to the location; it is enough if it is a place she would like to be so much that she can see its details.

I Am Up in the Mountains

I am all alone
studying about how many times a
star twinkles in a minute.
I'm up in the mountains.
I love the howls of the coyotes
and the wolves.
The trees blow up in the mountains.
When I look up at the stars
it looks like when I was a baby
and had a mobile over my crib.
It had a moon with stars on it.
It played music.

—*Laura K.*

I am riding horseback on a beach
the water is lapping at my horse's feet
my hair is blowing in the wind
I hear the ocean coming in
and my horse's feet clomping at the sand
my horse has no saddle
palm trees are on the side of me
their leaves blowing in the wind
in front of me all I see is sand

—*Erica K.*

Use Your Schizophrenia

I have a confession. I like the *National Enquirer*. Not a lot, mind you, but you have to admit, a newspaper that can come up with *Hateful Little Chemist Poisons Chubby Wife* and *Unsuspecting Sunbather Bursts into Flames* deserves downright admiration. My affection for the *Enquirer* has grown into something of an addiction. In Woodstock, a village of spiritually upwardly mobile souls, it's okay to call in sick because of a bad Tarot reading. It's not okay to stand in line at the grocery store reading the *Enquirer*. I'm the lady disguised by a Hawaiian-flower scarf tied around her head wearing black motorcyclist wrap-arounds, the one with her nose plastered to page four, reading about how a mob nearly removed the eyebrows, chin, and one ear of an actress who plays the part of a truly evil mother-in-law on one of the soaps.

Fascinating.

Of course, if you think about it, it was easy for that angry mob to confuse the actress with the fictional character she portrayed. Knowing nothing about the actress as a living person, and knowing a great deal about the character the actress played, was all it took to replace one with the other.

Just as it was easy for the angry mob to confuse the actress with the soap-opera character, it is easy for many readers to confuse the poet with the poem's narrator.

Sometimes, indeed oftentimes, it is not wrong for the reader to assume that the person speaking in the poem is the author herself. Many poems are exactly about the author's particular, peculiar experience or idea or dream. Lots of poems are a crying out, filled with outrage or longing or enthusiasm or anguish, straight from the throats and the real lives of their makers.

A great many of the poems students write fit this bill; they are based on actual experiences and real feelings. These poems can be in the first person ("I trudge through the woods") or the third person ("she presses her nose against the mirror"). In choosing the first person, the author makes it clear he *is* the same as the narrator. If the poet decides on the third person, he's taking his experience as his subject while creating a distance in which to gain perspective. It is as though he were looking through the small end of a telescope.

The Sympathetic Experience: Persona

Fourth- and fifth-grade kids want to write about the events of their lives, from a solitary walk in the woods to almost drowning, and they want to write about the mysterious symbols of their dreams and fantasies. They like to read each other's stuff to discover in what ways their passionately felt experiences are unique and in what ways they are common to other kids'. Poetry is a means by which the author's experiences can be captured in words, preserved and shared. Helping a fifth grader realize that life is the stuff of poetry both supercharges daily, mundane events and alleviates anxiety over feeling inadequate in the face of making art.

As deeply into their own lives as fourth and fifth graders are, they are equally concerned with the experiences of other, different people. These kids really feel for other people, so strongly that they often cover it up with what appears to be scorn. The mockery of a popular child for a new kid in the class is really panic. What if the new kid displaces her position in the group? Or, what if her parents move and she becomes the new kid? Just as writing down an individual experience as a poem can help a child dwell in the richness of her own life, writing a poem from the point of view of someone else can help expand that same child's psychological awareness and sense of community.

Persona is the literary term for the speaker of the poem, different from the writer herself. A poem written in the first person, "I," in which the speaker is not the same as, but an invention of, the writer, is written from the point of view of a persona. *Persona* comes from the Latin and means "mask." Your kids will understand the word and the concept if you remind them how it feels to put on one of those very realistic Halloween masks, the kind that turn you into somebody else. When you create a persona and then write from that being's point of view, it almost feels as if you've left yourself behind and stepped into the skin of another life.

A good way to prepare for the meditation and writing of persona poems is to make an extensive list, either verbal or on the board, of lots of different types of people:

runaway	race-car driver
banker	diplomat
hairdresser	child lost in foreign country
shoe designer	librarian
single parent	horse trainer
organic gardener	compulsive liar
soldier	physical therapist
blind artist	widower
perfume salesman	doll collector

Play a game in which a volunteer becomes one of the characters from the list and has to answer a battery of questions hurled from all directions: What is your greatest fear? Where do you live? Why? What do you like about your life (job, family, etc.), and what do you dislike? What is the saddest thing about your situation, and what is the best? How do you plan to proceed with your life? What color socks do you wear? What was the last thing you lost? What are you most ashamed of?

In order to be three-dimensional, interesting, and worth paying attention to, a persona must have a complex life that the author is familiar with, even if a lot of the "facts" don't translate into the poem itself.

The following poem was written by an eighth-grade girl I worked with in Catskill Middle School. I often read it to my fourth- and fifth-grade writers for inspiration.

The Complaint

I'm stuck here but it's not my choice
I didn't come on my own
Yet my mailbox is empty
They've forgotten how to use the phone
Maybe arthritis has a grip on them, too.
Day after day I think of the days of raising them up
It's all I can do to keep from drifting off
These people who run this place
Have their own lives
But I don't really live
I'm just alive
There are others like me
But they sit motionless
For now I sit sucking on the dreadful smell
of medication
I observe the other crippled hands and weak eyes
Every day a little bit more of me fades away
when I leave here I won't even know it.

—*Eileen*

There is silence after I read this poem. Usually, after a bit, someone asks me to read it again. This time, before reading, I ask who the speaker is, what her complaints are, where she is. I ask how she feels, and how the reader knows it. I point out the fact that the entire poem is based on images—an empty mailbox, motionless people, crippled hands—and that the feelings of sympathy and empathy that rise in the readers come not because they are told how the persona feels but because they are graphically shown.

Johnny

Johnny spent his time in the
local 7-11
playing video games and smoking
his parents didn't care
alcoholics
that's what they were
Johnny came and went as he
pleased he had no curfew
wild, reckless

Johnny left for a year and
came back
They told him to stay away
next time
Johnny did.

—*Peter M.*

Nobody Cares

In the morning I walk to school
All by myself
I walk into the classroom
And I see everybody talking to each other
I sit in my seat
And I see people staring at me
I go to sharpen my pencil
But I just get pushed aside
Then we go to lunch
A gruesome ugly place
I see all fifth grade classes
Just sitting around and staring in space
At 11:30 we go back to class
I put my coat in my cubby
Wishing for a better tomorrow.
At 2:00 we get ready to go home
When I get outside
I walk home all by myself
And stay in my room for the rest of the day.

—*Eric B.*

The Mechanic Man

The mechanic man with long
swift fingers dirty and greasy
getting pinched every second
can't have a chance to
have lunch
can't even sit
down for a
minute you have to
work every
second
and you have
to do it on time

—*Dorian B.*

Dorian's interesting use of the second person here allows us to feel that he is standing inside the mechanic, and telling us with the colloquial "you" what it is like. At the same time, we feel the author to be standing in close proximity to the mechanic and addressing him directly with the pronoun *you*.

Jump

I am a person
living in an apartment
Kids live above me
They are like jumping
machines working twenty four hours per day
They don't do anything else
Friends are over at their house daily
running and playing
I saw the kids outside
they said hello
They seemed like nice kids
I had asked them if they would calm
down on the jumping
Yes was the answer
but
as you know
kids will be kids

—*William S.*

And finally, in this poem, the author's absolute assumption of a character different from him in all ways is apparent. I am impressed with the strong, natural voice. We hear the syntax and language of an old neighbor, bothered by the noise but resigned to it.

Spiritual Connections

When I was in West Africa I had the great fortune to be invited to a day of celebration and tithing, given by the village healer, a very old, very revered woman with an elegant walk and a distant look in her eyes. The whole village turned out dressed to the tens, and the best drummers and calabash players were there. There was tieboun chienn, a rice and chicken dish, and many goats and chickens were slaughtered and given to the village poor. The drummers drummed a rhythm called Lamba, which belongs together with a dance whose steps progressively make you dizzier and dizzier, until you are flung outside yourself. It is a dance of healing and transformation. It was explained to me that each person has a spirit to whom they belong. The village healer helps a troubled person reconnect with her spirit, literally returning her to the source of vital energy and life. In our culture, when we are troubled we go to psychiatrists to discuss and intellectualize our pain; or we turn to alcohol, drugs, food—anything that will help us numb and sooth our panic. Personally, I'd rather dance.

By tradition and by function, a shaman is a highly respected spiritual healer, a doctor of the soul. As well, the shaman is the bridge between the community and God. The shaman knows how to speak to (the) Higher Being(s) and knows how to identify and translate signs. The shaman is the overseer of all ritual events—births, marriages, harvest, burial—and leads the celebration and the giving of thanks. As well, the shaman has a lot of political savvy, understands the nature of power, and is constantly watching for trouble spots in the community. The shaman is, in short, a leader, both spiritually and politically.

The following poems were written by kids after very passionate discussions about shamanism, culture, and community. With the meditation, I asked the writers literally to become members of a tribal community, participating in a ritual. They each assumed a persona; notice how sharply delineated and clear each persona is. Some kids became the shaman, others, the proud son or daughter. Some kids became a parent in the community, others, a child. Each writer was free to imagine the tribe as they wished; I didn't correct cultural misconceptions, or ask that the poems be researched to ascertain accuracy. What is "factual" about the poem is the degree to which each child writer is able to leave behind the trappings and assumptions of his own contemporary Western culture, and become someone else, someone truly different.

The Great Hunt

We were all gathered around our shaman on a dark night
All of us watching him dance to the Gods
Asking for weapons for the great hunt
He was dancing like a bird
But then we saw it
All sorts of weapons dropped from the sky
spears, arrows, knives
Then we bent down thanking the Gods

Our shaman handed us each a weapon for the hunt
Then our tribe set out to hunt the great white bear
Then we heard a roar
The ground started to tremble
Our tribe ran in fear
And I was the only one left
I only had a spear and a knife
But I knew I had to kill it
So first I charged it with my spear
It threw me back with its huge claw
Then I threw my knife into its heart
It fell in agony
I knew I had killed it
When I brought it back to my tribe
They made me chief.

—*Terrence A.*

The Shaman

Midday by Big Rock
we are dancing for
success.
We ask for luck
from the spirits
of long ago.
Our shaman is
trying to levitate
into the sun to make
our request.
Our shaman is wearing
bright yellow pants
and an orange sun
on the front of his
shoes.
We do this ritual
on a clear day
before the end
of the world.
If we are not
successful, our
shaman will
die and be
transformed into
the sun.

—*Betsy H.*

My Shaman

My shaman is dressed
in black robes and has black
slippers that look like a crow
fluttering in the air on a
dark winter night. There is a
fire burning and people banging
drums and people singing and
dancing and people watching
a bird twirl in the air and
then my shaman is gone

—*Glenn M.*

A witch doctor:
Is like a magician who could:
Turn a rock into a dove:
Fluttering off into the bright
Shining sky.

—*Joseph T.*

I hear a shaman, I hear a shaman;
There he is over the distant hills
talking to the gods.
I hear a shaman;
Begging his gods for water as they
slowly move across the golden
desert.
I hear a shaman; with a mighty
voice preaching to his weak & hungry
tribe where they shall settle next.
I hear a shaman. No!
I see a mighty shaman & he
is my father.

—*Greg E.*

The following poem, remarkable for its eerie, surreal concepts, was also the result of the same meditation.

We all awake with
our dreams floating around
us. It is a cold
gray night. We all still
dreaming get up
and walk around.

We write down
the end of our dreams then at
night we all try to
continue our dreams. They go
on and on
till we hear our leaders call us.
We proceed to dream till
it blurs
away and we are wide awake.
Every night it goes on till
we begin
another
dream. Each dream lasts a year.
We never have a nightmare.

—Danielle D.

Maybe you and your kids would like to choose a particular culture or tribe, and really research the subject. If you live in a community where the resources are available to you, you might be able to get your school to hire a musician or storyteller who works within a specific tradition. Organize an after-school reading that incorporates music and traditional dance, masks, costumes, and food, along with the poems your kids have made.

Place

Poetry by no means has to be about a human subject or even contain a human observer. A poem can simply be the experience of the world the poem creates and contains. Details of sense—whispers, a flash of light, the smell of rich soil, a harsh scrape—provide the poem with grounding. Such detailing brings the world to life for the reader and subtly suggests the vision out of which the poet writes. Details of sense—sound, smell, sight, taste, touch—collectively add up to a total impression of place. The reader is literally placed within the poem.

For kids, certain places are especially evocative. As adults, we carry the memories of our own childhood meadows and rambling closets and leatherette car interiors with us. When something reminds us of a cherished niche, we are suffused with emotion. I can't drive through Illinois without going miles and sometimes hours out of my way to return to Kewannee (Hog Capital of the World, incidentally, a fact of which I am inordinately proud). I wander back and forth between the church where my father preached and the tiny parking lot where I recall our enormous house once stood. I look at the shaky fire escape hanging from the Sunday School door and see my redheaded friend Mary Ellen eternally dangling, her feet slipping between her scabbed knees as she executes skin the cat, once more and always. My heart slams as I tip my head back and peer up at the grated landing, because I know she will fall, even though she never does and, in fact, is probably at this moment chasing her own tribe of redheads out of an oak tree, where they practice their own version of skin the cat.

Some kids like dark, secret places. Underneath the bed, behind the couch, in Mom's big, musty closet. Other kids like to be high up, perched on the sharply slanted roof of the house, at the top of the Ferris wheel, balanced on the top rung of the silo. Some kids like creeks and rivers and oceans, others like the lush green earth. I ask meditating kids questions pertaining to the quality of light, the atmosphere (temperature, weather, etc.), what draws their attention (such as fireflies or a shout), what is constant (lapping waves, the cloudy sky, the ticking clock, etc.). I tell the kids to put themselves in a place where they can see the outer limits. For some, it will be a small place, like the coal room of an old house; for others the "limit" they observe might be broad, like the horizon where the ocean and the sky stitch together. This approach will help you avoid poems that begin, "My place is in New York City."

Another way to approach the subject of place, is by asking your kids to imagine a large place, like New York City, and then progressively tighten the lens. Where in New York City? A block that is bordered by a park. A park that contains a pond and a playground. A swing-set upon which lots of kids climb and swing. The light brown scar of earth that is beneath a particular swing, where the feet of the swinger scrapes the grass away. Conversely, the lens of place can begin very tightly focused and gradually widen.

My Greenhouse

As I was walking
through my greenhouse I noticed
it was dark.
I said what a beautiful sight
Seeing the stars
and the moon and all the pretty
flowers. Then I
walked in my house and looked
out my window

I saw my greenhouse. It looked
beautiful the next
night the moon was full and
my flowers bloomed

—*Nicole E.*

Sneaking Peeks

I don't know how it happened, but in one class during the group discussion we all admitted to each other that we . . . well . . . we like to walk around at night and not really *window* peep, but . . . um . . . kind of look in. When we finally all forgave each other for our obviously marred upbringing, then we could really get down. We talked about looking at how people kept their houses, about how they decorated, about what we liked and didn't. We talked about those little mysterious moments framed in the yellow light of a window, about how intense they are because the night is so dark it seems to erase the outer world until only the world within the house seems real. One kid told about seeing two people slow dancing in an utterly silent house; try as she might, she could hear no music. We talked guiltily but with (I'm sorry) true pleasure about overhearing people fighting (it's juicey; admit it, you like it too)—and besides, it makes our own lives seem more bearable. Then after we had talked, we wrote poems about window peeping.

Window Peeping on a Blue Night

I am wandering
through my backyard
I look in my neighbor's
window. It is tinted a bit
But luckily I have good eyes.
I see a light
go on in the kitchen.
Somebody walks in crying
In my heart I am asking myself
What's the matter with her.
She is mad, a fierce grin on her
face. Her kitchen is blue tinted
floors. She sits down. My mom calls
Danielle Time to come in.
So I run in my house and go up

in my room close my eyes
and dream.

—*Danielle D.*

Danielle's use of the color blue reminds me of something from Picasso's blue period.

And Little Places

Poor, misunderstood haiku. Let's be honest, we've all done it at least once; given our class the Haiku Assignment. Goes something like this:

> **Write a poem in three lines. You are allowed five syllables for the first line, seven for the second, and five for the third. You must include an indication of the time of year as well as the time of day; your poem should give a strong sense of where the speaker is. Please include in your final line an image that is so earth-shakingly mind-blowing it will force the reader to perceive life with a new-found spiritual depth that cannot be verbalized. You have ten minutes.**

Get my drift? Even if you leave out the requirement of catapulting spirituality, it's still weird. What's wrong with it? What's wrong with it is the fact that we are ignoring the inextricable relationship between language and form. Japanese haiku has all kinds of requirements for which we have no equivalency in English. They consist of seventeen "onji," which are sound symbols and not the same as syllables. The seventeen sound symbols in a traditional Japanese haiku each receive equal stress. The only way to do that in English would be to compose an entirely monosyllable poem, and even then, you'd have trouble. Don't panic, I'm not going to tell you not to let your kids write haiku. But loosen up a little about it.

When I do this writing assignment with my kids, I don't think of the poems as haiku. They are little poems with big meanings. They are close-ups of objects and actions. Because they are so physically small, they have to use the fewest words possible to get a particular meaning across. If you want, give your kids some formal requirements. The authors of the following two little poems were pretty rigid about sticking by the five-seven-five syllable count, because the class had done extensive work of this order before I arrived. We made a deal, whereby they could keep five-seven-five (sounds like plant fertilizer) but substitute words for syllables counted.

I split this particular class into three groups. The first group began by writing a little poem about something they could see at or inside of their desks. The second group began by writing a little poem about something they could see while laying on their bellies someplace in the room. The third group began by writing a poem while standing or sitting by the teacher's desk. We figured out a system of rotation, so that each group wrote poems from all three perspectives. This turned out to be a really interesting assignment. By the end, we all realized that where you are has everything to do with what you experience.

I remember this class period in almost surreal detail. The class, a small, shy one, worked in utter silence and concentration. I played a tape of whale songs to contribute to the mood. I had brought in some pink carnations for the kids and for their teacher, because they were one of my all-time favorite classes. As you will see, the fragile, transitory petals were a source of inspiration. These small poems are so delicate and so sturdy I admit I get filled up with gooey pleasure each time I read them.

> Blue vase stands on desk
> Pink flowers fall to side of vase
> Leaves die in the heat.
>
> —*Emily F.*

Desk

> The desk is very still
> As people slither by along fast
> A person is writing poems
>
> —*Rachael D.*

And Surreal Places

I spent one pleasant but misguided year trying to learn Chinese. I had been seduced by the majesty and subtly of the poems of Li Po and Tu Fu and a myriad of others. The translations I had read all seemed so stiff, except for those by Kenneth Rexroth, which had a grace that made me hungry to read them in the original. There were two things I wasn't bearing in mind:

1. I had studied French, Scots Gaelic, American Sign Language, West African Woolof, a tiny bit of Spanish, and English. The only one that took was English, probably because that's the language I go shopping

in. When it comes to learning foreign languages, I am beyond bad. I am pathetic.

2. Chinese is visually and aurally pretty; which, coupled with the fact that I have an admittedly over-developed imagination, spells doom. While my classmates spent hours committing the characters to memory, chanting the ten thousand words they would have to know to be conversant, I sat doodling characters which I saw as little, individual stories, and cooing their names with mindless delight. I had a lot of fun that year, but not much sunk in.

Recently, I was going through my books, and my hands fell upon a collection of Chinese poetry. The left side of the page contained the poem in Chinese, the right, a translation of the poem and commentary. I studied the Chinese side to see what I could remember, and was a little chagrined to discover I remembered only the character for *man* because it looked like a little guy racing for the bus. As I looked at the characters one by one, my old bad habits took over, and pretty soon I was giggling wildly at the bizarre story I saw hidden in the words.

Needless to say, I Xeroxed the poem and handed it out to my kids the next day. I told them they had to translate the poem, that I didn't have the slightest idea what it said. They had a riot with it. Here's the original and two of the translations:

> The tall man limped down the street for he had high heels on his feet. A dog ran out into the rain for he had bitten a man on the leg. The dog bite did not hurt so the man had stumbled on the dirt and he almost ripped his own shirt. He fell on a line of people he left behind. When he got up he fell back down and waked no more to the store.
>
> —*Dwayne the Great*

Dwayne the Great did some nice cross-cultural footwork here. Can you tell by reading his piece aloud that he's a school-famous rap man?

Chinese translation

As the sun rises above the mountains, the wind whistles and howls furiously. The hinges on the rusty old water pump cough and wheeze like an old man. The light dances on the water and shimmers like gold. The scarecrow slowly hides away as his straw disappears in the wind. Posies grow among the blades of grass by the old barn, its red

見咸陽橋牽衣頓足闌道哭

哭聲直上干雲霄道傍過者

問行人行人但云點行頻或役

十五北防河便至四十西營田

paint chipped off. The old farm house's light shines through the window as the warm fire blows against my frozen body. The sands in the hour glass slip through each other going to the bottom and once again the moon meets the sky.

—Jennifer S.

Incidentally, I use no meditation prior to writing these translations. I give the kids a lot of freedom with it. A character can mean a single word, or ten words, and some characters can be meaningless, that is, they make no picture as far as the translator can see. Those meaningless, uninspiring characters can be skipped.

Moving

"The poems your students write are really moving," my mother told me. We were sitting in her living room, with pages scrawled on by big loopy aqua pen-marks scattering the floor like confetti. Me being me, I spent the next couple of days contemplating the metaphor. Moving? What a lovely way to name the emotion. When something moves us we literally are taken to a new place, we are transported, and, in the trip, transformed. It's motion, literally, something that cracks open our incredibly dense noun-ishness and infuses us with the energy of life. It moves us to feeling, to action.

I met one of my best friends at an all-night contra dance in Brattleboro, Vermont. A few times a year, several hundred people get together and do the dancing our great-grandparents did when they were flirtatious and young and brimming with life. We dance from eight o'clock at night all the way through until eight o'clock in the morning. It's an incredibly moving experience. You push through exhaustion, through irritation, you push past thinking you should be at home doing something practical, like washing the sheets, canning the tomatoes, curled up under the feather quilt. By two in the morning, you're so hungry you have a flash of becoming hysterical, but you push past it. By four o'clock in the morning, all your little human anxieties have nestled down, and you feel sweetly in love with the world. The fiddles sound like cicadas, and the room is literally so humid from everyone's sweat that everywhere you look there are halos. Your eyes can't rest on anything for more than a moment, because the caller tells you to "Ladies'-chain" or "Swing your partner," and you are off and whirling, your feet contacting the ground only in order to lift you off of it. You feel no resistance, but just the ease of moving along in the stream, going with the literal flow.

It was just about this time that I met Rick. He grabbed me when the caller cried "Balance and swing," and he swung me so hard my feet lifted off the ground and I flew through the air.

"Hi," he said. "I seem to have turned into a verb."

I informed him that he was now officially one of my best friends, that we could skip the part about getting to know each other. That was five years ago, and he's still a verb, and he's still one of my best friends.

Really, it's important to remember that absolutely everything is in fact, no *thing* at all but a motion, an action, a living relationship of constantly changing parts. Even a rock is s-l-o-w-l-y moving, its atoms swimming around their nuclei. Movement is sacred; it's the getting from place to place. Without it we ossify.

The same is true with language. I have said again and again that it's important to find the most specific verbs. Sometimes, the most specific verbs are the most metaphorical, because no word exists for what you are trying to say. You have to root around in your experience and find something unusual and unexpected that will shake your reader into the vivid experience you are trying to convey. This year, a fourth grader asked me if the most specific word was the same as the *true* name for it!

One of These, Two of Those

I cheered at length in a previous chapter over Natalie Goldberg's book *Writing Down the Bones*. For those of you that missed the plug, rush out immediately and buy this book. It is high-energy and fun and full of great insight and utterly inspiring. I was shocked and delighted to discover both she and I, two teacher/writers who had never even heard of each other, had similar writing projects. She suggests listing ten nouns on one side of a page. On the backside, you choose a job and list ten verbs that go with it. Then you try to hook the nouns with verbs that are unusual but that work. One example she gives is "The lilacs sliced the sky into purple." It's a great way to get your mind thinking about what actions are really appropriate to certain nouns.

My assignment is similar. Here it is:

On the board, make three columns. The first column will include nouns. The second will include specific verbs. The third, nouns again. Take suggestions from the kids to fill each column:

Noun	Verb	Noun
grass	humming	night
air	singing	day
dog	leaping	foot
feather	quivering	lion
whisper	sneering	pot
fog	lifting	pebble
rug	sniffling	tree
smoke	cracking	cradle
Kleenex	dropping	sneeze
chair	swinging	shoe
glass	boiling	egg
pond	fretting	soap

Take one from column A and combine it with one from column B and one from column C. You have a noun-verb-noun phrase, but the first noun and the verb link up to become an adjective describing the final noun: "a fog singing day"; "a Kleenex sniffling sneeze"; "a kiss swinging cradle."

Your kids will discover poetic images and unusual phrases that will startle the imagination.

Incidentally, I owe thanks for the inspiration for the this assignment to a seventh grader named Ray who misunderstood another assignment and came up with the following poem. It is a brilliant capturing of what the first ache of love is like.

Bizarre Love Story

One air humming night,
A harsh breeze whipped my tight cold skin
A young girl I seen walking with the wind
A strange ache was occurring to my weakened knees
We sat on a bench a stare came about.

—Ray J.

Following are excerpts from two poems that resulted from this assignment. In this particular class, after making the lists on the board and talking at length about possible combinations, the kids closed their eyes and visualized themselves moving through the woods.

My Walk in the Woods

It was a leaf crunching day
in the Spring. I was in the woods

full with thundering green
trees. (excerpt)

—Martin A.

A Walk in the Woods

One day I was running fast in a huge field.
While I was running
the flowers were babbling to bloom. (excerpt)

—Angela F.

It's hard for fifth graders to grasp the noun-verb-noun phrase. Martin's poem begins with the correct arrangement ("leaf crunching day"), but his really brilliant image is a verb-adjective-noun combination ("thundering green trees"). Angela's stroke of genius likewise doesn't fit the noun-verb-noun prescription ("flowers were babbling to bloom"), but it rivals anything that Dylan Thomas ever wrote. Remember: there are no mistakes in creative writing. Creative writing time in the classroom should not be used to reinforce other classwork concerning grammar, spelling, and so forth. You can certainly point out, gently, that these combinations are different from noun-verb-noun, and ask who knows why. You can certainly suggest to a writer who has completed the first and second draft of a poem or story that before it gets hung in the hall she should check words whose spelling she isn't sure of, so that other people can read it and because she must be pretty proud of her work. But please don't become upset at students who didn't follow directions. In creative writing, the ultimate direction comes from the writer's own interior.

Organic Gardening

Poems take time to develop. They begin someplace deeply buried in the author's experience. At first they aren't even verbal, but merely an urge, a sense, an atmosphere so rich it takes hold in the subconscious and begins to grow. Poems that have deep roots will be impossible to forget; poems whose sources are shallow will be easy to uproot and discard.

All parts of the poem are organic; they develop in relationship with all other parts, and cannot be predetermined. Even the form of the poem, the way its lines fall upon the page, the untouched spaces of white between stanzas, has an organic quality. This is true even in set forms, sonnets, villanelles, sestinas. The form is the architecture, the armature, which hammers out a felt space in which the poem is free to unfold. It's like a soft canvas bag whose shape is determined by what it contains.

This is a very hard thing for a child to grasp. It takes a leap of faith, and a certain amount of courage, to really write a poem. In truth the only rule is, write exactly as you are compelled to by the poem that does not yet exist. You, as teacher, must help your kids trust their instincts, hear their own voices, still their nervousness about their creative impulses. If you do it enough, and with encouragement, they will understand. The poems they write will be beautiful and harsh, subtle and passionate, personal and universal. The work a teacher does is the same as the work a parent does, is the same as the work your young writers are learning to do: to love, and in the loving, to accept something so utterly that it cannot help but reach its fullest, most brilliant potential.

The Body

The body of an ocean is the waves crashing against the sand. The body of an ocean sounds like a human snoring. Hee-hoo hee-hoo.

The body of the ocean is the waves swaying from beach to beach. The body of a poem is the lines starting from one sentence to another, going back and forth with many or few words.

The body of a human is not just what you see on the outside but what you feel and sense coming from the inside. It is a lot like a poem because a poem comes from the inside, your heart and soul.

—*Tara F.*

In the end, our children are our sweetest poetry. In teaching them to cherish their words and visions, we teach them to cherish themselves.

6

Fourth- and Fifth-Grade Fiction: Crazy Quilts of Life and Dream

Getting Inside

"Excuse me, are you the writer?"

First day in a new school; I seemed to be going the wrong way. The entire corridor overflowed with kids surging with the mindless conviction of salmon going upstream to spawn. It was hard to make any progress at all. I was afraid of smashing little feet in neon high-top sneakers. And besides, there were so many of them I was literally borne along.

"Yeah, I'm the writer."

Deep sigh. "I need help." She squinted up at me hopelessly. "Plus, you're going the complete opposite direction. I'll walk you to your room and tell you my problem." She shoved her glasses up on her nose with a jelly stained thumb, patted her Afro, grabbed three books that were about to slide out from the pile in my arms, spun me around by the hand, and led the way. As we walked, we talked.

"I have a story."

"Great. You want me to read it?"

"I haven't written it yet." She twisted her hair. "It's in my stupid head and I can't get it out."

Boy, do I know that feeling. She talked and I commiserated. Stories aren't so hard to think up, we agreed, but they are hard to manage and control. Characters sit there like boring guests; you can't picture where they actually are, and nothing happens. When you finally have the whole thing written you go back and reread it, and it doesn't feel right. Everything is out of order; too much was said in one place and not enough somewhere else; and nothing sounds natural.

"If it's so frustrating," I asked her, genuinely curious, "why do you want to do it?"

She squinted up at me, and then her eyes got a faraway look.

"Because," she said carefully, "when I just think about it, the story has an inside. Nobody but me knows about it. When I'm writing and it's coming out good, it feels a certain way. Like I'm inside the story. Then when I show it to Lisa and Jade, they can go there."

She wasn't in any of my classes, so we met during lunchtime. We talked a lot about her story and about how to "get inside" it. For the next few days I would see her hunkered over her notebook on the top step of the stairs, or leaning against the tree on the playground, staring at a spot so far in the distance only she could see it. Then, on the last day of my residency, I glanced out the window of the teacher's room to see three little girls piled together, reading over one another's shoulders with a shared expression of rapture. A few feet away, the writer shoved her glasses up on her nose with her thumb and grinned.

Losing Control

Stories *are* hard to manage and control. So don't, especially at first.

In the process of writing, the story unfolds. It isn't the writer's job to use the force of will to *invent* (from Latin, "to come upon, to find") the story. The story is something the writer comes upon as it finds its own way to the surface of her consciousness. Sure, she needs to be willful, disciplined, determined, even controlling, but that comes later, in the process of fine-tuning the piece.

It's okay for the first draft of a story to be wildly out of control, illogical, sloppy, and inconsistent. Like life, sometimes you have to try a thing out a couple of different ways before you know what will work. As I was working on this book, I moved into a cabin buried in the woods. I had to paint the place, hang shelves, make curtains, and settle in. The cabin is extremely small. The kitchen holds an antique trunk and a wobbly table. Above it, tucked under the eaves, is a sleeping loft, *à la* Little House on the Prairie. There's hardly room in which to sit up. The living room houses a desk, three bookcases, a teeny pine dresser, and a twig rocking chair made by hobos during the depression.

No sooner did I get my house squared away, than I got a blinding vision of how it ought to be. Nevermind that I had only two weeks to finish the first draft of this book; nevermind that the cabin is too small to move around in much less rearrange; nevermind that I had just gotten everything unpacked and settled and the place looking livable. Nothing would do but for me to stop everything, then, there, and redo it. By nine AM the place was in shambles—open drawers, furniture piled into corners, pictures unhung, cabinets unscrewed from the walls. By three PM I was crying and cursing myself. I had created a mess, and the only way to salvage it, it seemed, was to put it back the way it was. But I forced myself forward, and by eight in the evening, everything was done, just the way I wanted. Before, it was satisfactory. Now, it's wonderful. Before, the desk was in a dark corner. Now, I sit in a full flood of sunshine, which flutters through the trees just outside my big window.

The metaphor is obvious. I had to get all my stuff into the cabin any old which way so I could see what it looked like and feel how it should ideally be. The way I first organized things was the rough draft of my living space. Then I had to do the work, the rewriting. It was a mess and I wished I didn't have to do it, but something was driving me. The results were everything I had envisioned. Same goes for a story. The rough draft is just for getting everything out of your head, any which way, and onto paper. After that, you can cut it up and rearrange it, draw arrows in purple ink all over the text, add things, change things, merge two characters, delete three, and end it differently.

First the vision, then the revision.

The World Teems with Characters

The most basic elements of the short story—character, setting, and action—are the building blocks that contain and convey all the complexity, grace, elegance, drama, and subtlety of the greatest stories the world has ever seen.

At their most basic level, stories are about what happens to somebody. Certainly the issue is more complicated than that: they are also about the position the narrator takes, the angle of vision, unspoken meanings, the beauty of the language in which they are told. Experimental modern fiction has even, at times, done away with character and/or event entirely.

Still, stories that come from the heart have as their pulse human passion, experience and imagination. As you and your students explore the fictional mode, the best place to begin is with characters. Human nature in all its variations is what compels us to keep making and listening to stories. The earliest known myths explained the operations of the universe by way of a pantheon of gods whose all-too-human personalities conflicted and combined in endless variety.

Much of what occurs in a story depends upon the nature of the person to whom it is occurring, or, conversely, who is making it happen. Kids, in their earliest fiction-making efforts, tend to ignore their characters rather rudely, treating them as paper dolls rather than as proxies for people. They charge madly through the beginning of their tales to arrive, breathless, at what they consider the real meat—what happens.

But in truth, there is no such thing as "what happens." There is only what happens to whom, and why.

Getting to Know Whom

Most kids are natural interrogators. Everybody knows an old person—a grandparent or great-grandparent, an elderly neighbor, even the clerk at the corner market. Everybody has a natural curiosity about the past, about "when you were a kid." Instruct your children to interview an older person. Here are the rules for interviewing:

- Ask for a story about one thing that happened once. If your interviewee gets off the subject, gently return to the event by asking another question about it, specifically.

- Pry for details. If your grandmother tells you about how she met Grandpa, ask what she was wearing, how she wore her hair, what she liked best about Grandpa.

- Stop your interviewee whenever you have a further question about something.

- Remember to listen carefully to how your interviewee speaks. You can use it in your writing.

Your students can either take notes, use a tape recorder, or simply listen. Remind them, however, that notes are just a brief list of single words and phrases to prompt their memories later on. They are not a word-for-word transcript of the interview.

Your writers can bring their notes to class the following day. In class, ask them to write the interview in the following way:

- Write the story your interviewee told you.

- Do not use the word *I* or *me*. You may, however, use *my*. (This allows for "my grandmother" but does away with "told me that before I was born . . . ," hence, keeping the focus on the true subject.)

- Remember to use specific verbs and nouns, even if your interviewee didn't.

- Fill your story with details. If your interviewee couldn't remember a detail, then you must make it up. Remember to close your eyes and picture the details you make up, before writing them down.

- Use your five senses.

- Think about the way this person talks as you write the story.

Here is an example written by a fourth grader:

How Grandpa's Fortune Slipped Through His Fingers

In 1916 in the middle of World War One, my grandpa was five at the time. It was in Schenectady N.Y. He and his grandfather were planning to go to the store in the afternoon. My grandpa walked beside his grandpa pulling his red cart. When they got there his feet were aching. His grandpa bought a watermelon and put it in the wagon. When he was home my grandpa wanted to be helpful. He lifted up the watermelon. It slipped and landed on the floor instead of the counter. His grandfather got very angry. Years later when his grandpa died, he left his fortune to a little girl next door.

—*Rebecca C.*

Invented Characters Based on Fact

Once your kids have learned to write about characters they know from real life, they are ready to create characters. Believable characters, however, have a grounding in reality. A story about a bag lady who rolls her eyes around in her head and mutters to herself doesn't allow for much reader sympathy. A story about a bag lady who will not talk to anyone because years ago she was betrayed by a friend who did not keep a secret, invites the reader in to share emotions.

Bring in a stack of photographs from your family album or cut from magazines. Before passing them out, lead a group brainstorming session. Together, make a comprehensive list on the board of all kinds of personalities. Your list should be almost absurdly complete:

affectionate	jealous
sloppy	foolhardy
gallant	dishonest
sly	petty
narrowminded	meek
flirtatious	sentimental
cautious	modest
enthusiastic	selfish
organized	considerate

Discuss these different types, and talk about what kinds of reactions people in the class have to certain types. Be careful to avoid the obvious—nobody likes someone who is selfish or jealous—by asking a volunteer in the class to defend a mythic character with these traits. Asking a child to understand and explain another's negative trait is the first step in encouraging your children to really understand the lives of the characters who will propel their stories forward.

Now, pass out one photograph per child. Ask each writer to study the person's expression, gestures, clothing, hair, and sitting or standing position for clues as to what kind of person they may be. Stress that you are interested in only visual details and facts pertaining to the photograph, even if they are invented by the writer. You want to avoid something like this:

> This lady looks like she is mad. I don't know why she is mad. I can't see who she is mad at. Once my grandma got mad at me because she said I dumped over the garbage but I didn't, it fell over by itself, I wasn't near it.

The above piece is about the writer, not about the photograph. The following is more the sort of thing you're looking for:

> The old woman has just slammed the screen door. Her gray hair is falling out of its bun, but she doesn't notice. The wind lifts a piece of her hair and in the backyard it blows against the sheets. One sheet has fallen but she doesn't notice. Her shoulder hunches over. If her son turns around to wave she will wave back. Otherwise she will just stand and stare as he marches down the road.

In this version, the writer implies, and the reader deduces, that the old woman is distracted and stubborn. There is the sense that there has been some kind of difficulty between the old woman and her son. Potentially, it is the beginning of a story.

Here is an example of character developed by this technique:

Farmboy

> He is sitting on his horse. He is a short chubby kid. He lives on the countryside. He has feet that are all bunched up from walking barefooted. He has short brown hair that is always messed up. At night he dreams that he is riding his horse into the sunset. He has a very good sense of humor. He wears a pair of bluejeans everyday with a red shirt. He always loses his key to the house but the next day he always finds it. He does not feel bad about losing his key because he always finds it the next day . . . . He has an older sister. He doesn't like her that much because all she ever does is talk about boys.
>
> —*Jessica M.*

Strangers

Ask your students to observe a stranger, mentally noting details. Later, in a different location, they will write down as many details as they can recall. After they have finished writing, ask them to change some details and to feel free to add some things that weren't there at all. Were you studying a serious man in a gray suit sitting at a table? Give him a newspaper and a chattering, distracting companion. Maybe the fluffy teenager you watched in the grocery store line would be more interesting in a different outfit and carrying a little poodle.

You will find that some students will write with an omniscient (all-knowing) point of view. This means that the narrator (the "voice" who is telling the story) has access to the mind and heart of the characters. Other students will choose simply to observe behavior and appearance.

> A girl named Kathy had shoulder length greasy blond hair. When she was younger her mother abandoned her. You would often see tears coming out of her brown eyes. Though she tried to forget about this she couldn't. Now she lived with her grandmother and grandfather. Her aunt lived with Kathy too. Kathy's aunt's name was Laura. Laura and Kathy were both age eleven. The house Kathy lived in was just the right size for her. The yard was too, but she didn't really like to go outside. She'd rather stay in and play with her dolls, write a story, or sing. Kathy sometimes liked to play with Laura. Some of the time they would fight. They really didn't get along too well, even though

Kathy's grandmother thought they did. They were completely different from each other. Kathy could write good, Laura couldn't. Laura talked back to her mother. Kathy wouldn't dare do that. She wanted to get on the good side of her grandmother. Sometimes Kathy's grandmother would be very nice. Then Laura would come along and ruin it. You could tell that Laura was jealous of Kathy, but Kathy wanted them to be friends. Sometimes she cried in her room, but whenever Kathy was around anybody but her grandmother, she would hold it in. (excerpt)

—Marjorie V.

Family

Every member of your class lives with at least one other person, and has grandparents, aunts, uncles, cousins, or miscellaneous extended family members to study. Every family has its stories that are told and retold so many times they become part of the fabric of family life. Ask your kids to write down a story about something that happened to a member of their family. This writing will be facilitated by a quiet meditation beforehand; your kids will discover they have a multitude of stories inside they didn't know were there.

When my mother was pregnant with my younger sister Lauren, and I was an inquisitive toddler, my mother was boiling water for tea. Not a big deal, but the incident that took place in that harmless-looking small yellow kitchen has been burned into my memory for life. As she was taking the saucepan off the burner, she tripped on one of the pot lids I was gleefully throwing out of a low cabinet. I remember a scream, my mother falling and the pan of steaming water being splashed onto her side, and my father rushing to rescue her from damaging her precious cargo. As she limped down the basement stairs to cry, I whimpered, "Mommy, Mommy," and waddled after her. "No, Nora," my father said, scooping me up in his arms, "leave mommy alone. She needs to be alone for a little while."

—Nora M.

Nora's crafting of this tiny story is remarkable; she might be only nine years old, but her masterful control of style and language blows my mind.

Mom and I were in the garden. She told me about when she was a kid. She said she thought she looked funny when she was little because she wore braces. I was just about to say if I were there I don't think she'd look funny. But she told me not to talk. So I didn't. She said a kid told her she looked funny. But then daddy walked along

and slugged that kid. Mom was so astonished that she hit the guy
dad had slugged and by the way the guy's name was John. John was
so astonished that he fainted. And mom & dad dragged him to the
garbage can, it was just big enough for John so mom & dad took him
& threw him in the garbage can. Well that's that said mom and left.
Mom and I were just about finished with the garden when she was
finished with the story.

—Jennifer

Jennifer wrote from the first-person point of view. What results is a
story within a story. On the most obvious level, her piece is about what
happened to her mom when she got braces. On a subtler level, it's about
Jennifer's relationship with her mother ("I was just about to say if I were
there I don't think she'd look funny. But she told me not to talk. So I
didn't."). But what is marvelous about the piece is how the two time
frames are joined together. The girl, who is felt to be about Jennifer's age,
throws her tormentor into the garbage, says, "that's that," and steps
across the decades into the second time frame, the one in which she is
adult and Jennifer, the child. Jennifer's crafting of her mother's past and
their shared present, in such a way that they finish simultaneously ("Mom
and I were just about finished with the garden when she was finished
with the story") provides the reader with a double satisfaction, having
been told two stories at once.

Ask your students to remember a moment in which they have simply
observed a member of their family. This piece of writing will involve a
single point in time and a single observation. The writer can choose either
the first-person point of view or the third. In the first-person point of view,
the reader will feel an intimacy with the narrator. There will also be the
sense of two characters (as in Jennifer's piece above)—the narrator and
the character she observes. In the third-person point of view, the reader
experiences a greater sense of objectivity.

My grandparents died only a week apart. I couldn't bear to go into
the funeral home but at last I did. I didn't want to go near the coffin
but when I did I saw my grandmother, she was wearing her red dress
she never wore and her real pearl necklace. She was holding her bible,
a rose was on top of her bible. She had seemed like a mother to me.

—Michelle L.

Michelle's piece, from the first-person point of view, gives the reader
a strong sense of intimacy thwarted, of bereavement.

Weirding Out

Claudia Lewis's book, *A Big Bite of the World,* contains a story written by a young writer who uses the phrase *sneaky baby.* The phrase hit my funny bone. I pictured sneaky babies taking over entire towns when the grown-ups go to sleep. Fourth- and fifth-grade kids, I'm happy to report, share my giggliness concerning sneaky babies. I don't know what it is that gets to me, maybe something about the sound of the words, coupled with image—innocence and evil. A personality sketch of a sneaky baby, shy lion-tamer, murderous clown, or any other weird type is a fun way to explore the territory of character:

> Sneaky babies are bad little babies they come out at night and go marching down the street with tambourines in parents' best clothes.... Sneaky babies get out Dad's wallet after his paycheck and play poker. (excerpt)
>
> —*Karen L.*

Setting the Story Down

The world brims with settings, locations, places. Everything is someplace, and nothing is no place. If a story doesn't have a location where it can be found, it can't really exist, even in the reader's mind. Something that cannot be found anywhere isn't real; it's phantasmagoric and will disappear from the mind with the rapidity of dissipating fog. Stories, being in truth nothing but a collection of words that refer to a vision existing in the writer's mind, must be made as real as possible in the reader's mind. Setting grounds the story, gives it weight and dimension, and makes it feel real to the reader. It also contributes to the overall sense and atmosphere of the story. It can be used to underscore and emphasize the story's action (your typical midnight rainstorm as the murderer moves through the darkened house) or as an ironic counterpoint to it (your typical carnival music and laughing crowds at high noon on a bright sunny day someplace in the innocent Midwest, as the murderer moves toward the Ferris wheel).

One of the earliest tasks the beginning fiction writer faces is learning to verbalize the setting, which is essentially visual. Meditation is especially useful here. Every conceivable setting is literally bursting with a multitude of details. It is not the writer's job merely to describe the setting, for to describe it accurately and thoroughly would be to create a monster.

The writer must first attend to all those details and then select from them. He must decide in what manner, both spatial and temporal, to compose them.

A simple, peaceful meditation about an evocative memory of a place will provide images and details for writing. Some students will write pieces that do not deviate from the actual experience:

> It was a cool, clear summer night and I was up in my treehouse watching the sun go down. The sky was beautiful colors. It was full of light blue, purple, orange and red. The sun was setting to a fiery red. The moon was full and rising up to be a deep orange with some red. The sky was turning electric blue. My treehouse is in a large oak tree. In the woods behind my house, I could see the construction site. Children were playing ball in the street. The moon now fully up was spreading a soft light on everything. The street was getting quiet as kids went inside. A squirrel ran by with its cheeks full of bread. Down below a dog was chasing a chipmunk. The air started to smell like someone was barbecuing or burning leaves. The streetlight started to flicker on. A bluejay flew by with a worm in its mouth. Some people were jogging in the construction site where new homes are going up. My friend's moving van was driving up the street. I came up here so no one can bother me. (excerpt)
>
> —*Jessica K.*

Others, natural dramatists, will immediately leap through a familiar setting into a story replete with exciting action:

> I am trapped in a deep dark mineshaft. I am not able to tell the time of day. All that is around me is inky blackness. With my hands I can feel the sharp edges of the rocks above, below, and in front of me. A constant drip drip drip sound can be heard. Though it is faint the bare walls of the cave echo it back and forth as if they were playing ball. It is cool and damp and on many of the rocks water can be felt. A dank wet smell is present in the small chamber. I can feel the closeness of the walls as if they were slowly moving inward. Many of the rocks have skinny crevices spidering all through them. Moss grows on some, but most are bare. I got trapped in here when my friend pulled a rock out and caused an avalanche. I can hear him now scraping at the wall of dirt and rock. (excerpt)
>
> —*Eric S.*

Setting and Incidental Action

You can approach the basics of setting with your kids in any number of ways. A meditation during winter about a private, beloved place in the summer can yield good results. Working from photographs or paintings is another possibility. Or ask your kids to keep a setting notebook in which they write a single paragraph setting description each day of any odd place that suits them. Under the kitchen sink, the candy aisle in the grocery store, the view of the fair from the top seat of the Ferris wheel, the inside of an old car at the dump—the odder it is the better.

More ideas: grab a single setting, as small as a closet or as large as the playground in the park. Observe it from day to day. A bedroom cleaned on Sunday will gradually accumulate dirt and mess by Friday. A plate of food left uneaten in the refrigerator (or for those with truly tolerant parents, in the garage) will mold and rot in colorful, interesting, and constantly changing ways. The view of the street from the dining room window will be very different during a rainstorm than at high noon on a sunlit day, different during rush hour than at dawn. Weather changes things, as does the writer's mood, as does what occurs in the setting at any given point in time.

After your writers have become comfortable with writing about pure setting devoid of action or character, ask them to remember a single, simple journey. It can be no big deal, such as a car ride through the country, or sitting in the dentist's office. The emphasis is on the place, not on what happens there. Again, meditation is useful here, with you, the teacher, as prompter, suggesting that they look again at all the details of the place:

The Walk in the Park

One day I got bored, so I asked my mom if I could go to the park and she said yes.

I was not wearing any shoes. I got there and the ground was muddy.

I walked along the path that was there. I heard water. I got closer and closer to it. When I got to it, there was a beautiful waterfall. It was getting dark, the sky started to get very dark too. I forgot I heard on the radio that a big storm was going to hit.

As I was walking home, I spotted a glass. It had cracks all over. It was all muddy and dirty. I picked it up and inside the glass was an ant home. As I was holding the glass a lot of ants crawled up my arm. I threw the glass down and knocked the ants off my arm.

I started to walk back. Every step I took my foot sunk in the mud.

> When I got out of the park, I stepped on a piece of glass. As I was limping home, the storm hit.
>
> —*Kim G.*

Kim unconsciously composes the details of her piece in such a way that they repeat one another. The clear beautiful waterfall is echoed by the glass that she finds which is echoed by the sliver of glass she steps upon. Notice that her first glasslike image (the waterfall) is large enough to act as setting, the second image is small enough to be held, and the third image is so small it is a fragment imbedded in her foot. Furthermore, the mud that surrounds the beautiful waterfall is echoed by the mud that coats the glass. All the images coalesce as the splinter enters her muddy foot. The fact that Kim did not intellectually establish these relationships in her composing of the piece only serves to underscore my point that writing is a process of discovery, and the strongest writing discovers relationships the subconscious already knows.

What You Know Plus What You Make Up as You Go Along

So far I've been talking about using real-life everyday experience for a story's setting. Makes sense; places culled from real-life have built-in details, evoke feeling in the writer (and done right, in the reader), and will help the writer envision the unfolding of the story. But don't get stuck in reality. Everybody likes to daydream, and everybody bases daydreams to a large degree on stuff they know. A fisherman will fantasize the perfect catch, a dancer will daydream herself into prima ballerina-hood. The fisherman's images will include a lot of information he is expert at; lures and water temperature, weather and his ability to stay still. The dancer ditto; her wild (mental) leap to fame and fortune is due to her arabesques and turns.

Chances are about 100 percent that you've got a class filled with experts. The wonderful part about it is, everybody's expertise is different. Some kids are fascinated by motorcycles and cars, others by the cultural aspects of motorcycle gangs or the fifties (I was crushed when one little guy sporting a ducktail asked me to tell him about the old days). Some kids know a lot about fish aquariums or skinning a deer; others prefer to talk about preparing a morney sauce for bananafish or embroidery. Feel free to explore, and exploit these special interests. Encourage them to daydream themselves into a setting they know a lot about. Science, history, biography, social studies can all be enhanced by encouraging your kids literally to experience a vision concerning them.

> I live in a hut that I made by hand. First I broke off branches and put them into the ground, then I found some leaves and vines and used some elephant tusks for decoration. There is a land of the dead. Where I live when elephants or other dinosaurs think they are going to die they go to the land of the dead and die, that's where I get my tusks and bones for my house or to bribe wild dogs. (excerpt)
>
> —*Jillian S.*

Settings of Magic and Absurdity

One of my favorite writing assignments involves the transformation of the mundane world into a world that is purely surreal. After a discussion and listing of numerous natural places, I ask the kids to put down their heads. They breath slowly and deeply, visualizing their rooms in detail. What objects are on the floor and on the dresser and in the closet? What colors are there, what do you hear? Suddenly, I suggest, the room begins to change. It's changing to a whole other place. I ask them to visualize how it changes. Some see an explosion, others, a gradual melting away. For some kids, the room becomes a grocery store or a shopping mall; for others, a cave or another planet. The setting that is real to them has yielded and led the way to a setting that is utterly invented. Furthermore, the peculiar and unexpected action of the room changing by itself excites the young writers to visualize the beginnings of story action. With this assignment, setting easily begets action:

> Last Tuesday I was sitting on my bed when the room was changing somehow. The dresser moved into the wall and bookshelf went into the floor. The bed turned over and was a fallen tree. Everything in my room had disappeared. I was in some woods with lots of bushes and trees. I walked around and touched things to make sure they were real. I looked inside the fallen tree and there were centipedes, ants, rollie pollies, small spiders and cobwebs. When I got up I heard some growling by a small green bush. I went to check it out. Then the door opened and it was my room in less than a second. My mom put some clothes on my bed. I asked her if she saw what happened. She said no, and shut the door, and it was the woods again. My clothes turned into snakes on the fallen tree. I looked at the same bush again and a big black bear with glowing eyes jumped out. He chased me around the woods. I climbed up a tree and sat on a high branch. All of a sudden I fell in the tree. I was falling for a long time. When I landed

I was in the middle of my room on my back. Everything was there. Even the clothes my Mom brought.

—*Mark S.*

Lights, Camera, Action!

As with character and setting, the best place to begin an examination of fictional action is with the writer's true-life experiences. Every kid in your class has a million memories and a million stories to tell. Everyone has been lost, been furious at an adult, been blackmailed by a sibling. Many kids have narrowly escaped death, have been to an exotic place, or saved the day in some way, shape, or form.

Prewriting meditation helps kids to envision something they can then write about; it also slows down the cascade of details that are already in place. Ask your kids to put down their heads, and then simply instruct them to remember something that happened to them one time. You can ask the entire class to meditate on a single, common experience, such as getting lost, or you can ask each member of the class to recall one intense event they lived through. Remind your writers to dwell on the memory, literally to return to it, to see it, smell it, feel it, hear it, and taste it again. Remind them to use specific verbs and strong nouns, and to write down any details that are important. You might want to read them the following example:

The Make-up Disaster

When I was 3 years old, or maybe 4, I'm not sure, well anyway, my mom was downstairs cleaning dishes. I snuck upstairs, found all my mom's jewelry, make-up, and old clothes, I put on the old clothes first, they smelled very musty. I took the pretty pieces of jewelry. I put them on. I looked in the mirror they looked beautiful. I took the make-up box, I pulled out the eye shadow. There were three colors, Blue pink, and a tan. I decided to use all three, one on top of the other. I took out the rouge, it was very messy rouge, it was like cream almost. I stuck all four fingers in it and rubbed it all over my face. I used every last drop of it. It was on my hair, my face, my arms, a little on the clothes, oh, even the jewelry was covered. Rouge was everywhere. Next I pulled out the lipstick I had a ball with that. When I finished, it was all over everywhere, the bathroom counter, the sink, the mirror . . . . (excerpt)

—*Mary Beth D.*

Listening Good

After your kids have written their real-life experiences, point out to them that they have written a story. Ask them who the characters are, and who the main character (protagonist) is. They will be able by now to explain the setting and what part it plays in the story. Several of your kids might want to rewrite their stories, because after they look at them with the eye of a literary critic they will see discrepancies in logic, undeveloped sections, uneven writing, or flat characters. Because they were there, however, they will have no doubts that they can rewrite the story with the richness and grace it deserves.

Writing about a real-life experience is also the easiest way for a writer to become comfortable with dialogue. Everyone who has ever read a transcription of the Watergate tapes knows that good dialogue doesn't exactly imitate real speech. It can't, or it would be peppered with *umms* and *errrs* and statements that are incomplete and contribute nothing. We ignore each other more than we listen in conversation, forgiving one another for piles of words and sounds that are random and rambling. Readers are not so forgiving, however. Dialogue, therefore, has to give the illusion of speech to be effective.

Memory is a natural editor; when a kid is laboriously transcribing all the important details of a remembered event, he is going to tailor his reported dialogue to convey information and a sense of the characters. He will do this without thinking about it. Dialogue is very hard for all writers, especially so for young ones. Graceful dialogue develops with experience and time. However, sometimes kids get to feeling stymied when the dialogue is stilted. I had the great good fortune to be in the right place at the right time and overheard the following conversation:

"My characters don't sound good when they talk. They don't sound like they really are talking. It's stupid." The writer chomped down on her yellow #2 pencil and glared at three other writers who were workshopping her story. The writers, one by one, made suggestions: could she skip the talking? Were the characters saying important stuff or just saying nothing? Were the characters talking too much? The questions were good, but the writer just became more and more frustrated. Nothing helped.

"They just don't sound good enough when they talk," she muttered once again.

A sage voice from an adjacent workshop group said, "Maybe you just aren't listening good enough."

Stretching the Truth

I like to encourage my writing students to fib magnificently, because a really good story contains a lot of stuff that never happened. A good lie is like fine seasoning: it's subtle. Your kids will get the idea of lies and fiction if you ask them to write a story about something that happened, sticking as close to the truth as possible. Then, ask them to lie. Change it. Here and there, just a little, nothing unbelievable or outlandish or inconsistent. Rewrite it as something that could happen, given the context of the story. Here's a great example:

> I can't turn my head, or stretch my back or move my hips or anything. I can just barely wiggle my fingers and toes. I don't know how I got in this laundry chute. All I know is I'm here, and I can't get out. I'm stuck at an angle with my head down in the dark, damp chute. It smells of sweaty clothes, muddy sneakers and faintly of the aluminum which it is made of. You can see the light rays glimmering and bouncing off all the little dents in the chute when you are on the 2nd floor looking down. But when you are stuck inside all you see is dark, dark, dark. You can't even see the light from the laundry room where it comes out. My palms are wet as I try to yell for help. My throat is so dry no sound comes out. When I think about if I'm hurt or not I can feel the close walls around me; pressing on my back and stomach. I cannot move my elbows. I must remember hard not to panic. I'm going to be sick. The blood in my head is pounding. My knees sting terribly. I have to turn my head but I can't. I try extra hard, pushing with all my might. My head finally budges, pushing my nose into the side of the chute hard. Suddenly my nose and lips feel wet. I stick my tongue out and catch a drop of the liquid. The taste is unmistakable; blood. My nose must be bleeding. "It's so dark in here," I think, then I realize my eyes are closed. When I open them, the walls of the chute are so close my eyes cross. I close my eyes again. "I'm tired," I think. That is my last thought before I fall asleep.
>
> —Kelly G.

Kelly's details are convincing because on some level they are all real. What is probably an actual experience (getting partly stuck in a laundry chute) is creatively expanded and developed. Kelly is careful to toss in a lot of realistic details of sense to ground the story. The result is a true piece of fiction, an invention Kelly stumbled upon as she overlapped her life experiences with her imagination.

Pure Invention

After your kids have examined character, setting, and action as discrete, separate elements, and after they have experimented with combining them into a story via their own solidly grounded memories, they will be ready to create a story from out of their own imaginations.

As your students meditate, ask them to visualize a basement in detail. Speak slowly, allowing them the time to imagine themselves moving to the stairs. The quality of light is important, as are the objects in the basement. Ask many, many questions. They move up the stairs and onto the first floor. Room by room, meditatively move them through the house. Up the next flight of stairs. Up to the attic. Ask, always, that they see objects, colors, smell, feel. You can suggest there is someone unknown in the house with them. You can suggest they are with a companion. You can suggest they are looking for something specific. What is it they are looking for, and why? Each time I do this meditation with a group, it comes out differently. When they reach the attic, they discover something. What? This is a long meditation, and it is essential that you give them time to visualize all the changes you suggest to them.

The stories that result will come easily to your students. They have just had a vivid and affecting mental experience, and they will be anxious to write about it. You might want to play some quiet classical music, or get a recording of Andes flute music (it's enchanting). This assignment is easy for the writers in spite of the fact that it is a complete invention, because the protagonist is someone with whom they share a complete common ground of experience—themselves. You will find some horror stories, some pieces of romance, some adventure stories.

The Aging House

I woke up in a cold basement and I was 3 years old. Then I started to walk around. There were old paint cans, old wallpaper, lumber of all shapes and sizes, clothes from the year of the flood, and detergents. The smell down there was a cross between TIDE and mothballs. I wasn't very scared I had been in scarier basements before. I looked out the window. It was warm and sunny out. It was so nice that I ran up the stairs to play in the yard.

Then I walked into a kitchen. I was 12 years old. This was weird but fun. There was a cake, mugs, and a coffee pot on the table. The same smells were in the room. It was a very nice kitchen. There was a new refrigerator, stove, sink, and cabinets. When I undid the blinds and looked out the shiny glass doors it was dark and gloomy. Almost like the beginning of March. I was curious to see the rest of the house.

Then I turned left into the kitchen. As I did I became 20 years old. The living room had brown velvet furniture. The carpeting was beige. There were brass lamps on glass tables. Trophies and medals stood on one shelf. On another were pictures of flowers. The room smelled like fresh roses. Then I opened the heavy cotton drapes. It was snowing out. Everything looked so beautiful.

Then I was walking up soft carpeted stairs. When I finally reached the top I was 30 years old. The hallway had a hard-wood floor and pictures of birds on the walls. The room had windows. I saw two bedrooms.

One was yellow with baseball stuff all over. The other one was pink with stuffed animals. A bathroom was grey with flowered tile, a grey curtain, and a grey and blue floor.

As I was walking I heard tiny footsteps. Then I started walking up attic steps. The steps were narrow and creaked with every step. As I was walking I grew to 40 years old. I opened the attic door.

The attic was a regular sized room with light blue walls. The room was bright and sunny. I knew this room before. Then I remembered. It was the room when I was 10. Then I unpacked a trunk on the floor. All my old things were in it. Then the door flew open and my dogs stood there that died when I was 5. I cried at all the memories. Then the tears turned into my pool. I was 10 again. (excerpt)

—Jennifer H.

The Total Story

Once your kids have achieved a degree of comfort and technical control with setting, character, and action it's time to encourage them to explore the total story, using their own taste and judgement in how they choose to play the basic story elements in relationship to one another.

A lot has been written in recent years stressing the importance of using the events and experiences of a child's own life in writing. I agree that a child will write with more authority and deeper commitment about a subject he has personally experienced than a subject he is completely inventing. But, for kids, as for adults, stories mean invention as well as biography. A young writer's commitment to a story does not necessarily begin and end with experiences she has personally gone through. Fiction is grounded in our psychic realities as well as our socially shared ones; fears and expectations, frustrations and unexpected surprises all take on symbolic forms to people and propel kids' fiction.

Your writers will come to you throughout the school year with ideas for a story that are directly gleaned from something they are living through. But as well, they will come to you with the request that you lead them in a meditation so that they can explore comedy or horror. The following writing ideas involve worlds of absurdity, comedy, and fantasy. Because they are fun to imagine, fun to write, and fun to hear out loud, your kids will willingly and lovingly embrace them. Don't limit your writers by insisting that every story have something that really happened as its impetus. Instead, allow them the freedom to explore worlds they can only enter through their imaginations. Through the meditation work, their visions will be strong and committed; and through the experience of writing, their stories will be strong and true—even the ones that take place on Neptune.

Witches, Giants, Cottages & Beans: An Update

Fairy tales are part of our culture. We all know the ins and outs of Cinderella and Little Red Riding Hood and Hansel and Gretel. We all remember how strongly we related to the children in fairy tales when we were young: talking animals; words or foods that act as charms; the fact that time stands still for some characters and not for others—it's magic to our hearts. There is always the threat of evil and the satisfaction of seeing it vanquished. Bruno Bettleheim, in *Uses of Enchantment*, discusses the cultural and developmental necessity of fairy tales in fascinating depth. Every fourth and fifth grader knows fairy tales are for babies, and every fourth and fifth grader harbors in his secret heart a nostalgic affection for them still. They represent the time when he was innocent and young.

Familiar fairy tales offer a pre-established story line and structure that can easily be tapped by your kid writers. Brainstorm and make a list on the board:

Little Red Riding Hood	Rapunzel
Cinderella	The Princess and the Pea
Snow White	The Three Bears
Jack and the Beanstalk	The Red Shoes
Sleeping Beauty	Hansel and Gretel
The Three Pigs	Rumplestiltskin

Beware! *Pinocchio; The Lion, the Witch and the Wardrobe; Star Wars;* and *Gremlins* are not fairy tales. Your kids will ask why. Say to them, "You ask too many questions." If they persist, point out the fact that true fairy tales are inherited generation to generation. They don't have a single author, and oftentimes they have several versions. They involve magic, poison food, castles and cottages, and children as heroes. They are brief (so much for Pinocchio) and do not contain numerous adventures. Good prevails over evil. For your own edification, read Bettleheim.

With the class, discuss typical settings involved in fairy tales. The basic overall setting offers an indeterminate time in the distant, medieval past, which contains carriages, horses, hearths, one milk cow per family, a big black kettle stirred over the fire, and/or a magic mirror. Carriages, hearths, and the like have pretty much gone by the wayside and have been replaced by subways, cars, microwaves, convenient food marts, TV dinners, and makeup. We don't have kings and princes to throw fancy dress balls, at least not in this country, but we do have an upper echelon of political and economic society. We've got discos, videos, roller skates, punk hair, sushi bars, silos, newspapers, aluminum ladders, and all kinds of other junk.

So, what happens if you rewrite a fairy tale? Keep the accouterments (a poor, beautiful, good girl, her wicked stepmom, her crummy sisters, a really gorgeous guy, a shoe) but give them a contemporary veneer. Change the setting to Central Park or a farm in Vermont or a Honolulu beach. Give the fairy godmother a face-lift. Why not? She deserves it. Your kids will have a blast with this assignment, because they know what happens next, and therefore they know they can't go wrong.

Let the kids make up their own fairy tales. Start with a long list on the board of things and characters that are typically found in a fairy tale:

talking animals	royalty
commoners	cottage
woods	hats
talking mirror	carriages
shoes	jackets
gowns	brooms
apples	biscuits
giants	time stops
step-parents	

Your kids can dig into this list and add to it anything they want. Their stories can be as long-winded, involved, and modern as they want, or they can turn out like a classical fairy tale:

> Once deep in a forest there was an old, tumble down cottage. In this cottage lived an old, ugly lady. She had warts and pimples and a big nose with a double chin and gray hair and dark black evil eyes. She was very very wicked and tried to take away the things that are precious from good people. Now way way way down at the other end of the forest lived a royal family. Well just that day it was the princess' birthday. The princess was beautiful. She had dark violet eyes that shimmered in the night, her skin was peach color and her skin as soft as down, her hair was long, dark, brown, and it shone in the light. Well her mother the Queen was very sick and she gave the princess her bracelet that she always wore. It had been with the royal family for centuries. It gave the person who was wearing it good luck and kept her safe. A few days after that her mother died. Well the old wicked witch, Dunree, saw this all in her crystal ball that she had swindled from a dwarf. Well just then the princess wanted to go to a fortune teller to see if her life would be long. So Dunree made a poster saying she was a fortune teller in town and hung it on the gate of the royal palace. The princess was delighted. The fortune teller said first I must be paid, you will have to give me your bracelet. The princess replied but this has been in the royal family for thousands of years. Dunree said give me the bracelet or no fortune. The princess said take the bracelet. Dunree began the fortune; of course, she was lying. She said the princess would have a wonderful life. On the way out, the princess fell down the stairs and hit her head on a rock and she never got up again, but dreamed forever.
>
> —*Emily G.*

The following is an excerpt. At this point in the narrative, we have an evil step-mom who gives the protagonist an endless list of petty and insurmountable house-cleaning chores:

My Horrible Death

> . . . When I got back I said to mom, "I'm going to pick the flowers." So I went out the door again and went for the flowers.
>
> Then when I got out there I seen a baby bird, when I went to pick the bird up because of his wing being broken. After I got over to him he turned into these 2 hands that were grabbing for me.
>
> They almost got me but I ran back toward the house. But all of a sudden another pair of hands reached out for me. But I screamed &

ran west, but there was another pair there so I turned around and there was another pair there so I was surrounded by hands.

All this time I was screaming my head off. Then all 4 sets of hands were coming toward me. I couldn't run anywhere so I had to let them get me.

They all started eating me. I was screaming and yelling but suddenly my voice faded away and there was nothing left of me except my hair.

My evil step-mother thought something happened so she went to find me. She got out there and she found my hair and the little bird was there again so she went over to pick it up and it turned into the hands but she did the same as I did and them evil hands ate my evil step-mother all up except her hair and that was the end of me and her.

—Tabatha V.

Dreams

Fairy tales offer young writers a narrative structure, and at the same time, their weird nature encourages imaginative play. Dreams can also be used as a point of beginning and inspiration, offering, if not a pre-established formal structure, a familiar format. Both fairy tales and dreams take place in a world that does not imitate the world of the here and now; the writer is free to experiment with all kinds of outlandish, surreal, and fantastic inventions.

Get your kids involved in a discussion about dreams. What can happen in dreams that can't happen in real life? You'll notice some overlap with the sort of things possible in a fairy tale:

talking animals	people turning into objects
mind reading	walking on water
floating	objects acting alive
breathing under water	defying laws of physics
flying	objects changing shape, size

When your kids meditate this time, tell them to visualize a place that is like a dream. Repeat the list several times in differing order. "What do you hear? What else can happen? See it clearly, study all the details. Anything can happen, anything you want." Avoid using the word *dream* as much as possible. When the meditation is finished, ask your kids to write down the crazy, otherworldly story they just saw. There is only one rule. Don't end the story with: "Then I woke up. It was only a dream."

Dream stories can be very brief and as richly detailed as prose poems, or they can be developed to include several scenes and transformations. They have as their primary feature an intense atmosphere, a style. They can be hysterically funny, terrifying, or melancholy:

Crazy

I'm walking in a field. Then all of a sudden I trip over a rock. I find myself in a rock path. It leads to a maze built of bricks and cement. I make it to the end. I find myself on a beach surrounded by stone and wood mountains, and start to walk. I stumble over a crystal sundial pointing to the east. I turn myself facing the east. But all there is, is water that goes on forever. I hear voices in my head yelling and screaming. (excerpt)

—*James D.*

The Big Broccoli and the Headless Teacher

One day it was sunny then it was pitch dark. I lit a match then I knew I was wearing a pink dress with baggy arms and a pink collar and small little buttons all down the back. Then broccoli was chasing me. I was wondering why but then I remembered that that was the broccoli I didn't eat last night then it said eateateateateat I said ho crap I ran for a half an hour then I ran in my house and locked the door then I saw my teacher she said you didn't do your homework but her head was off then I took out my father's gun and said get out she went then I went to school and she had stitches all around her neck and she said did you have a good night's sleep and then she laughed I said hoooo crap and ran out of the room.

—*Sean K.*

What Happens to the House at Night?

Fourth and fifth graders love writing and reading stories that ooze absurdity. These stories work as long as they are grounded in a vision; for this reason, meditation is an essential prewriting tool. Without a strong grounding in scene, event, and character, wildly imaginative stories lack the tension necessary to propel them forward. They can easily get bogged down in their own weirdness and quickly collapse like a party balloon that has been stuck with a pin.

However, with the experience of writing a few pieces of well-grounded absurdity, your students will take off on their own. They will find, in their daily lives, all kinds of situations that can be stretched into the realm of the truly bizarre or ridiculously comic.

For example, what might happen at night after everyone goes to bed? Anything is possible. Remind them to use a wide variety of verbs (otherwise, you'll end up with stories in which everything is punching everything else), and to be specific with both verbs and nouns. Discuss the fact that in a good story everything that happens, happens for a reason. One catastrophe in the story leads to another, and that, to the next. Even the most ridiculous, surreal stories have some kind of operating logic.

The Night House

Just after I got home from trick or treating I went upstairs. It was late. I was very tired. I ate a few pieces of candy then went to bed. Right after I fell asleep my parents' clock radio walked into my room and said, "It's okay everybody come out he's asleep." My shoes started walking out the door yelling, "Let's party!" Then my clothes, my games, my calendar, everything in the room jumped down and started running after my shoes. They also were yelling and screaming. My parents were out on the patio while all this happened. In my parents' room all their stuff was jumping and laughing and talking. Downstairs in the kitchen the toaster was dancing with the coffeepot. The refrigerator was talking to the table. All the food was hopping out of the refrigerator. The stove was standing in a corner all alone. The sink was dancing with the microwave. In the livingroom the chairs were talking and the couch and piano were dancing. Upstairs I was waking up. I started walking downstairs, I walked in the livingroom first. I was hiding behind a plant and a stem started punching me and covering my eyes. He yelled "he's awake, hide everyone!" He let go of my eyes and I ran out to get my mom & dad. I told them what I saw and they went in the house everything was normal nothing was moving. They said, "You're crazy nothing's moving!" "Everything was," I yelled, "they were! I promise!" "Well they aren't now," my mother said, as she poured a glass of milk for me. The cup jumped out of her hand. "Oh my!" she yelled. "I told you," I said. Then everything started moving again. "Stop," my father said. They did.

"I give you my permission to party only at night, during the day you are to stay as quiet as possible and act like you're dead." "Okay" everything yelled. From that night on everything was good in the day, but at night, that's a different story.

—*Mary Beth D.*

Exotic Pets

Know why kids love pets so much? Yes, partly because Mom usually feeds them, walks them, vets them, and cleans up the occasional mess, leaving the kid with no actual work. But it's more than that. Kids haven't lost the ability to communicate with the animal world, and they can think of nothing better to do than go for long rambling walks through the neighborhood with Rover, or curl up for a cuddle with Friskie. I hold dear the memory of my brother at age four, leaning up against the side of the house shoulder to shoulder with Spot, sharing an ice cream cone. Brother took a lick, dog took a lick, back and forth, until Mom caught on and flew out the door to collar them both.

Because they love pets so much, and because as a group they own every traditional pet from cat through parrot, your kids will like to consider life with a pet nobody else is likely to have. Make a thorough list on the board of everything you can think of:

penguin	rhino
giraffe	bat
elephant	llama
centipede	octopus
ostrich	kangaroo
3-toed sloth	tortoise

These stories can be realistic or can contain crazy magic. Some of your kids will write them in the first person and others will prefer to cast someone else in the role of the protagonist.

Once there was a boy named Alex who wanted an alligator. Since his parents wouldn't let him have one he was very sad for weeks and weeks. One day when he was trotting down the beach he tripped on something. It was a little square box with a red button on the top. He pressed the button and a beam came out and hit a shell. The shell became huge. Then he noticed a little switch. He pushed the switch and pushed the button. The beam came out and it hit the shell and it was small again.

So the boy went to a dark and scary pond where lots of dangerous animals lived. He saw a big big alligator coming out of the slimy green pond. It was covered with green plants and gook. So he aimed the little red box at him and pushed the switch and pressed the button. He couldn't find the alligator. He got down on his hands and knees and started to look. Suddenly he felt something bite his finger. He picked up the alligator and put him in his pocket and went home.

When he got home, he put the alligator in an old peanut butter jar and went to sleep. Later that night he heard a scratching. He got up and looked at the jar. The lid was off and the alligator was gone. Alex looked all over for him. He went to the kitchen and saw him eating an egg. There were 22 eggshells on the floor. He quickly picked up the shells and put the alligator in his jar and brought it to his room.

He accidently pressed the red button and the beam hit the little alligator and he began to grow. But he didn't just grow to normal size. He grew as big as the house and his legs and arms and head were all sticking out the windows. Alex flipped the switch and pressed the button and the alligator didn't get any smaller . . . .

Alex could only do one thing so he flipped the switch and aimed the box at himself and pressed the button and he grew as big as the alligator and they both walked away and nobody knows where they are to this day.

—*Aaron L.*

Letters of Apology

Creative writing should serve practical as well as creative purposes. A young writer's new-found facility with language, for example, can help her impress people, make friends, make money, or get off the hook. We all make mistakes. There isn't a person in the world who hasn't broken something, acted irresponsibly, failed to fulfill an obligation, or otherwise blown it. People with self-respect and dignity fess up to their mistakes. They apologize. It's not only the mature thing to do, it's the smart thing to do, because if you ask, you'll probably get forgiven. I've discovered, in my own experience, that I'm forgiven more thoroughly if I explain why I blew it. In fact, the more details I offer the one against whom I've transgressed, the quicker I get forgiven. Now, if you think about it, you will realize that no mistake is so grave that an excuse cannot be found. True, you might have to lie; but in really dire circumstances, like for the sake of a really good story, I think its okay to call upon all kinds of disasters, natural and supernatural, from fire to insect invasion to malaria to mudslide, in order to explain why you forgot to walk the dog or can't find your homework. If you are clever enough, Dear Whoever will be laughing so hard by the time he finishes reading your letter of apology, he won't be able to remember anymore what he was mad about.

Dear Mrs. Janderson,

I'm extremely sorry that I was in your house yesterday without permission. However, I was not, as you said, stealing your antique lamp. What happened was this.

I was walking home from school, and all of a sudden this gigantic kangaroo came up to me. As you know, I was a kangaroo for Halloween and I still had my costume on.

This kangaroo must have thought I was her baby because she put me in her pouch. It was really hot in there and wet. There was hair bristling all over me and I couldn't see a thing. I kept bouncing around in there for over an hour.

Finally, the kangaroo let me out. You should have seen me run! I looked around. That kangaroo must have been some jumper because we were in a place I'd never seen before. It looked like a jungle. There were lots of plants all over the place and it was very hot and sticky. I was amazingly hungry and I began to think my trip had been longer than I thought.

I found a strange purplish fruit and gobbled it up. It tasted about as good as the sole of my sneaker. That fruit must have been magical because all of a sudden I was hurled into the air. I was pushed by an unseen hand over hundreds of miles. After a few days, I landed right through your roof. The roof caved in and I grasped your antique lamp for support. Then you came in. I really didn't mean to cave in your roof or to break your lamp. You understand. It might have happened to anyone.

Sincerely,

—*Sarah B.*

Dear Mrs. Masington,

I'm so sorry that I was unable to keep my appointment with you at school on Tuesday.

I started out to get in the car, but as I opened the front door of the house, it fell off in my hands. Being unable to leave the house thus unguarded I had to call the repairman. I reached for my cordless phone—what a jolt I received! My hair stood right up on end as blue waves of shock pulsed from the phone to my hand. My daughter saw me and, screaming, ran from the house. My neighbors thought, "Burglars!" and rang for the police. Meanwhile, I completed my call to the repairman.

Well, the police arrived about five minutes after the repairman, saw him working diligently and assumed he was breaking in. Just as he slipped the last bolt into place, they hauled him off to jail. Now I not only had to get to you, I also had to rescue him!

With my hair still on end, I left the house once more to head for the car. I pulled the car out of the driveway and into the street. Drivers' mouths dropped open when they spotted me, people screamed and drove right into one another. One motorist stared so hard he drove right into Mrs. Murphy's wash line. The car continued down the road sporting Mrs. M's flowered housedress.

Of course you know that to get to the school, I must pass the zoo. As I got to the gate, there were sixty elephants with picket signs blocking the roadway. Their grey, leathery trunks clasped signs which read, "we won't work for peanuts anymore!" As one of them reared up on its hind legs, I drove underneath him. Unfortunately, he didn't stay up quite long enough. He came down right on top of my car and now it somewhat resembles a pancake.

After the nurse encased my arm and leg in plaster (first she set the wrong ones and had to start over), I got in a taxi to meet with you. But the big, burly taxi driver thought I said "pool" instead of "school." He believed in direct delivery and drove me straight into the water. We rocked, rolled and began to go down with a "glug." We managed to squeak out just in time.

That's when the police showed up with the repairman in tow. With many shrieks and shouts, I was pulled from the pool and I identified the repairman for the police. They, however, were not amused by my quick dip in the pool and hauled me off for trespassing.

After spending the night in a dreary jail cell (I couldn't call, my one call was to my furious husband), I was released and sent home.

Could you possibly re-schedule the appointment—but come to see me this time? I'm rather afraid to go out.

Thank you!

—MJS

The second letter was written by the classroom teacher! I included it not only because it is a delightfully funny story, but to encourage you to write alongside your kids. They love hearing your work, too, and they are reassured when they see you writing. When you give them a writing assignment and then correct papers or visit in the hall while they write, they can get to wondering just how important, or easy, or fun this creative writing business is if you aren't interested in doing it, too. But the most important reason for participating in the writing is for your own satisfaction. You will discover, along with the kids, that the more you do, the better you get.

Grab Bag

Take several large envelopes. Mark the first one *characters*. Work with the kids in your class to come up with thirty or so people. Allow a separate scrap of paper for each character, and stuff the envelope with them:

ballet dancer	farmer
runaway	kleptomaniac
bank teller	artist
single mother	chef
carpenter	

Mark another envelope *settings*. Again, you need about thirty:

playground	bakery
bank	skating rink
badlands	fish tank
garbage dump	skyscraper
jewelry store	

The next envelope is the problem that is the trigger for the drama; mark it *action*:

a misunderstanding	a lie
stealing	a broken object
a broken bone	a broken heart
something lost	illness
having to move	

Keep this final category vague; it is up to the writer to interpret it specifically. Each writer takes one slip of paper from each envelope. Each writer can return a slip of paper once and try again, and it's fine to let them trade with each other. Interesting combinations will suggest themselves: a painter who becomes blinded at an art show, a banker tempted to participate in a robbery at his own bank. Some combinations might be outright weird: a ballet dancer who loses something in a fish aquarium. Your kids are allowed to change any of the details they wish; the idea isn't to follow the assignment strictly, but to use it as a jumping off point in the making of fiction. Don't attempt this assignment until your kids have been writing comfortably for some time. Once they feel in control of technique, they will be inspired by the possibilities.

If you wish, you can include another envelope that contains genres. Genres are types of stories. Different genres, as your kids will be quick to tell you, have to be handled in different ways. For example, you can't write a good mystery if everybody knows who-dun-it right off the bat, and science fiction needs lots of scientific detail to support the writer's claims.

mystery	ghost
romance	science fiction
adventure	comedy
tragedy	western
fairy tale	folk tale
tall tale	fable

If your students decide to write in a particular genre discuss with them beforehand what kinds of reader expectations they must deal with. Your kids might want to write two or three stories over time, in which two of the three elements are retained and the third one varied.

Culture

Many fourth and fifth graders are particularly interested in human culture. Culture is a complex and manifold issue. It includes how people behave toward one another, what systems of belief they follow, ritual and work, tools, food, clothing, entertainment. A child who has learned some facts about a culture vastly different from her own can use her creative abilities to identify with it and thereby come to a closer understanding. Conversely, any and all knowledge, whether scientific, social, historical, mathematical, or biological, can be used in the making of solid, grounded fiction.

Viking Women

One cold winter afternoon the Viking men set sail. They were looking for new land. Adventure was a way of life for the Viking.

All the women were at the ocean shore to say good-bye to their men. The women were left to take care of the village and the children.

After a long time the men did not return. The women decided to try to go after them. They took the other boat and filled it with all the supplies they thought they would need.

On a brighter clearer day they set sail. All the children were in the center of the boat. All the women were at the oars. They sang songs so that they could row together. After some practice they got pretty good.

A few days passed when they finally saw land. It was very pretty to see. The land was covered with pretty flowers of all colors. The water around the Island was so clear you could see the rocks on the bottom. As we came close to the shore the birds' singing got louder and louder.

We went ashore to see if there was food. Tall trees had bananas and some had coconuts. All you could hear was everyone's feet in the sand running to the trees for food.

From a distance we heard people's voices. We followed the voices till we came to an opening. To our surprise it was our men. Their boat sank in a storm and they had to swim to shore. (excerpt)

—*Debra D.*

If I was one of those Viking women, I think I'd want a letter of apology containing a better excuse than, "My boat sank"!

A Never-Ending Story

As far as I'm concerned, there is nothing better in the world than to be near a writer of any age who has just discovered the moment of "Eureka!" It's especially good when the writer is young, because what you are witnessing is a person discovering the point of perfect balance between mind and heart. As you watch her lost in her work, eyes studying a myriad of unfolding images you can't see, you just know it's a balance she'll keep forever.

The Girl and the Sea

The water rushed upon the big grey rocks and flowed gently back down. Lisa was sitting on the sandy shore thinking about how unfair and frightening her life was. Her little brother was sick and her parents were away, so she didn't know what to do. She picked up a pretty pink conch shell and held it up to her ear. Folks said that you can hear the sea rushing if you hold a shell up to your ear. She held it closer. Faintly, but she knew she did, she heard a small voice that came from the shell. Lisa, Lisa, Lisa, it called. Come here, Lisa. She was so startled that she almost lost the shell in the high rising tide. Walk, Lisa, Walk into the sea. Come live with us Lisa, Come. It lulled her. She walked cautiously in to the huge sea. The words echoed in her ears. The water came up to her knees, her waist, her shoulders and then covering her completely. She saw before her the most incredible castle in the entire world. Lisa walked closer to the elaborate castle. It was made of green glass with pink coral. The walls were slippery so no one could climb them. She opened the castle gates and a purple octopus took her coat. She walked slowly into the castle grounds. A whale came and led her into the most amazingly decorated throne room with pink and white coral. A sea horse led her through a long hall into a queen's sleeping chambers. The seahorse, octopus, and whale bowed down to a blue glass wall. The glass shattered. Out walked the most beautiful woman Lisa had ever seen. She had long dark hair tied up with ivory combs. Almond eyes and a small frame. She had olive skin and a fair complexion. Her dress was made of seafoam. Lisa bowed down to this enchanting woman. Somewhere in her heart she knew she would help.

"Madame, will you help me solve my problem?"

The queen made a graceful gesture with her hand. Almost instantly, three well dressed men in red suits with gold collars appeared. The queen said something in a foreign language that Lisa didn't understand. The men disappeared. Then she turned her attention on Lisa. "My child, what is it that you want? You have a problem, what is it?" said the sea queen.

"My brother is very . . . ." Lisa was cut off by three high pitched screams. "He's escaped, he's escaped!" Lisa looked around quickly. Who's escaped? What are they talking about?

The whale grabbed something out of an ivory and pink coral chest. "Lisa come ON!" Lisa stumbled through the castle gates.

As they were running they found a sly looking turtle. The whale took the object which turned out to be a golden wand. The whale touched each creature with the wand and they turned into something that could breathe on land. The whale turned into a fat husky sailor who had no hair. The seahorse turned into a sleek black stallion. The turtle turned into an ex-convict who had a wonderful sense of humor. The octopus turned into a woman doctor who stood up to no nonsense. The transformed sea creatures turned around and saw the sea queen running quickly to catch up to them. She murmured some words and disappeared. Out came a little white dove . . . . (excerpt)

—Lizzie S.

Lizzie wrote with total concentration throughout the period. Later, teachers told me she scribbled during study hall, wrote while she ate lunch, begged out of gym and sat in the corner to write. When she went home after school, she raced through her schoolwork so that she could get back to her folktale. She worked until she dropped with exhaustion.

She came to school the next day looking completely frazzled. Her hair stuck out in twenty-seven directions, her dress was buttoned crooked, and she had the sublimely contented expression worn exclusively by saints who've just worked a miracle and writers who've just finished a story. After class, she handed me sixteen pieces of paper scrawled on from top to bottom, in the margins—anywhere there was white space. At the bottom of the sixteenth page were these words:

> The End.
> PS. There really is no end to this story but for now, I will stop here.

She looked at me and I looked at her.
"Tired?" I asked.
"Yup," she said, nodding gravely. "And I never felt better in my life."

Writing, like living, is a process. To be done well, both require honesty, struggle, and a joyful embrace. Those who open themselves to the process of writing discover entry into an inner terrain that is continuous; a world truly without end. As your students' guide, help them to learn the journey well; and remember to learn from them, too.

Suggested Reading

From Teachers & Writers Collaborative

T & W offers a free catalog that lists over fifty books, tapes, and workbooks about teaching writing to children. Some that I've seen and found useful are listed below. For the catalog, write to them at 5 Union Square West, New York, New York 10003.

Collom, Jack. *Moving Windows: Evaluating the Poetry Children Write.* 1985.

Danish, Barbara. *Writing as a Second Language.* 1981.

Elbow, Peter. *Writing Without Teachers.* 1973.
Writing with Power. 1981.

Lopate, Phillip. *Being With Children.* 1975.

Nyhart, Nina, and Gensler, Kinereth. *The Poetry Connection.* 1978.

Padgett, Ron. *Pantoum.* 1989.

Penguin, Inky. *The Writing Book: A Workbook in Creative Writing.* 1986.

Sears, Peter. *Secret Writing: Keys to the Mysteries of Reading and Writing.* 1986.

The Teachers & Writers Handbook of Poetic Forms. 1987.

The Whole Word Catalogue 1. 1972.

The Whole Word Catalogue 2. 1977.

Willis, Merideth Sue. *Personal Fiction Writing.* 1984.

Ziegler, Alan. *The Writing Workshop.* 1981.

From Heinemann Educational Books

Heinemann Boynton/Cook offers an extensive and fascinating catolog containing books on whole language, literacy, reading and writing, rhetoric and composition, teaching English, and others. Write to them at 70 Court Street, Portsmouth, New Hampshire 03801 for a free catalog. Their published titles include the following:

Calkins, Lucy McCormick. *Lessons from a Child.* 1983.
The Writing Workshop: A World of Difference. 1987.
The Art of Teaching Writing. 1986.

Graves, Donald. *Writing: Teachers and Children at Work.* 1983.
Experiment with Fiction. 1989.

Grossman, Florence. *Getting from Here to There: Writing and Reading Poetry.* 1982.

Murray, Donald. *Learning by Teaching: Selected Articles on Writing and Teaching.* 1982.

Newman, Judith. *The Craft of Children's Writing.* 1985.

Ponsot, Marie, and Dean, Rosemary. *Beat Not the Poor Desk.* 1982.

Other Titles

Arnstein, Flora. *Poetry and the Child.* New York: Dover Publications, 1962.

Bettelheim, Bruno. *The Uses of Enchantment.* New York: Vintage Books, 1977.

Gardner, John. *On Becoming a Novelist.* New York: Harper & Row, 1983.

The Art of Fiction. New York: Vintage Books, 1983.

Goldberg, Natalie. *Writing Down the Bones.* Boston: Shambhala, 1986.

Klauser, Henriette Anne. *Writing on Both Sides of the Brain.* San Francisco: Harper & Row, 1986.

Lewis, Claudia. *A Big Bite of the World, 1982.* Englewood Cliffs, New Jersey: Prentice-Hall, 1979.

Rainer, Tristine. *The New Diary.* Los Angeles: J. P. Tarcher, 1978.

Rico, Gabriele Lusser. *Writing the Natural Way.* Los Angeles: J. P. Tarcher, 1983.

Index